She Was Only An Admiral's Daughter

A Comedy

by

HAROLD BROOKE

and

KAY BANNERMAN

GW00370987

SAMUEL FRENCH

LONDON

NEW YORK TORONTO SYDNEY HOLLYWOOD

one we do not fight alone! So stand firm on the promise and never give up on it no matter what obstacles the enemy places in your path... The palace may be just around the next bend!

Books, Tapes and Videos by Philip Cameron

Item	Price	Qty	Total
1. HOW TO GET <u>ALL</u> YOUR FAMILY SAVED (Paperback - 128 pgs.)	$7.99		
2. IT'S TIME—FOR HOUSEHOLD SALVATION (Paperback - 144 pgs.)	$5.00		
3. IS THERE NOT A CAUSE? (Paperback booklet -40 pgs.)	$3.00		
4. THE HOUSEHOLD SALVATION SERIES (6 audio cassettes)	$15.00		
5. THE HOUSEHOLD SALVATION VIDEO BIBLE SCHOOL. Six power-packed videos*	$99.00		

Sub-Total	
†Shipping and Handling	
Total	

*   Price includes study workbook.

†   Shipping and Handling: For items 1 to 4, please calculate the total price for these items and add $2.00 for all orders over $10.00 or $1.00 for orders valued under $10.00.
Item No. 5—please add $10.00 per set of videos ordered.

❑   Check here for a complete catalog of other ministry products including music, sermon tapes, videos and more!

Name_____

Address_____

City_____ St_____ Zip_____

Credit Card Orders—Card Type: ❑Visa ❑M/C ❑Discover

Signature_____Expires_____

Please send entire page to: **Philip Cameron Ministries,**
P.O. Box 241241, Montgomery, AL 36124, or call 1-334-277-9000.

If you have unsaved loved ones for whom you'd like Philip to join with you in prayer, please write their names here (you only need their first name) and their relationship to you.

Your prayer requests will be lovingly placed in our Prayer Altar, a replica of Noah's Ark (pictured above), symbolizing our commitment to agree in prayer with you till *ALL* your loved ones join you within the Ark of Safety, the Ark of Salvation, Jesus Christ. If you run out of room, add another sheet of paper then send your prayer list to:

Philip Cameron Ministries, P.O. Box 241241, Montgomery, AL 36124. For prayer call: 1-334-277-9000

Philip, please pray for my loved ones:

Example:

William   Cousin

_____   _____

_____   _____

Prayer List (continued):

_____   _____

_____   _____

_____   _____

_____   _____

_____   _____

_____   _____

_____   _____

_____   _____

_____   _____

_____   _____

_____   _____

_____   _____

_____   _____

_____   _____

_____   _____

_____   _____

_____   _____

_____   _____

_____   _____

_____   _____

_____   _____

_____   _____

Prayer List (continued):

_____   _____

_____   _____

_____   _____

_____   _____

_____   _____

_____   _____

_____   _____

_____   _____

_____   _____

_____   _____

_____   _____

_____   _____

_____   _____

_____   _____

_____   _____

_____   _____

_____   _____

_____   _____

_____   _____

_____   _____

SHE WAS ONLY AN ADMIRAL'S DAUGHTER

First presented at the Richmond Theatre
in 1971 and in the following year an extended
tour starring Leslie Crowther as Adam Dexter
and Dilys Watling as Polly Glover

Adam Dexter
Polly Glover
Walter
Beau
Mrs Darcy
James

The action takes place in Adam Dexter's bachelor flat
in London

ACT I   Morning

ACT II   A few minutes later

Time – the present

ACT I

Adam Dexter's bachelor apartment in a modern block of flats. Morning.

There is a living-room, a door into another room, off it a raised curtained alcove. The steps to it form a banquette and there is a wrought iron balustrade, curving round the balustrade and along the bedhead. The kitchen has a service hatch which closes down completely. There is a glass transom over the bathroom door. Beside the door, a laundry chute swallows the dirty linen with an appreciative gulp. There is a built-in clothes cupboard, a man's dresser and a mirror. The decor is trendy in the pickled pine, wrought iron and fur-rugged manner. The apartment door opens on to a corridor and faces another door, marked "Service".

When the CURTAIN *rises, the alcove curtain is drawn. The apartment is in darkness except for sunlight streaming through a crack in the sitting-room curtains. Walter enters in the corridor; he checks the number, rings the bell. He wears a suède jacket, cavalry twill trousers, crêpe-soled shoes. He looks exactly what he is—a well-set-up young estate manager. Polly Glover opens the alcove curtain. She is tousle-headed and pi-eyed with sleep.*

Polly All right—I'm coming!

Polly hurries through the door into the living-room, pulls the curtains back, sees the time

But he's early!

Walter rings the bell again. Polly goes to the letter-box, coos through it

I'm most awfully sorry but I seem to have overslept. Would you mind coming back later?
Walter Yes, I would. Let me in, Polly! (*He rings the bell again*)
Polly (*opening the door*) Stop it, Walter!
Walter (*taking in Polly's nightdress*) Ha, I woke you up.

Walter takes a step forward to give Polly a kiss, steps on her bare toe

Polly Woke me up? You've crippled me. How did you know I was here?
Walter Your brother Harry told me. (*Knocking over a small table without even noticing*) Not a bad little dump.
Polly It was until you got here. (*Picking up the table*) I think you've broken the top!
Walter Frightfully sorry.
Polly What are you doing here, anyway? I've never known you go further from the farm than the pub or the rugger field!
Walter I couldn't get you on the blower.
Polly It's gone dead. And don't sit . . .

Walter sits on her hat

Walter It's only a cushion.

Polly It is—was—my hat. And don't get to work on that pipe—you're scattering ash as though you were sowing seed in a turnip patch.

Walter knocks out his pipe on the ashtray—it breaks

Now, look what you've done!

Walter Frightfully sorry, Polly.

Polly And all over the clean tablecloth. (*She whips off the cloth and takes it through to the other room to the laundry chute*)

Walter (*following her*) Never mind that. Just get your stuff together and we'll be off.

Polly puts the cloth down the chute

Chute G-goign, g-boign, g-boign—GULP!

Walter Holy cow! What's that?

Polly The tablecloth on its way to the wash.

Walter Down there?

Polly Yes—the laundry chute to the basement.

Walter How do you get the stuff back?

Polly Washed and ironed at the end of the week. Now, Walter, I've got an awful lot to do . . .

Walter All you've got to do is get packed and come home—the Admiral's back.

Polly Daddy's come home? But he was meant to be in Gibraltar for the fortnight! What went wrong?

Walter The hotel! The first night they brought on the topless belly dancers, the next, the hall-porter tried to flog him his sister, and the third, he found the page boy in his bed. He's writing to the First Lord to tell him to pull the plug out and sink the bloody Rock. So get a move on or I'm going to get a rocket for leaving the farm. Old Daisy's due for the bull today, and you know what she is!

Polly I know what Old Daisy is—she's Daddy's prize cow and I'm sick to death of cows! And now, please go, Walter—I've got a date with a fellow.

Walter What fellow?

Polly I don't know. The Marriage Bureau's got hundreds on their books —and the computer's picked me out two.

Walter Computer? Marriage Bureau? What did you want to go and do a mad thing like that for? The Admiral will go ape!

Polly He's only got himself to blame. Ever since he bustled my sister and her boy friend up the aisle, all *my* fellows have just disappeared into thin air.

Walter (*squaring his shoulders*) I haven't disappeared into thin air.

Polly If you light that pipe, you will. You've got the pipe-cleaner stuck in it.

Walter Oh lor! I say, Polly, if you're so keen on getting spliced, what

about me? Only the other day the Admiral said I ought to get married—
good God, he probably meant to you! That's a jolly good idea. We'll get
married—O.K.?

Polly That's sweet of you, Walter, but it's not O.K. by me. I've got other
plans.

Walter Suffering cats, you mean you'd rather take pot-luck with a
Marriage Bureau than marry me?

Polly Yes. (*Hurriedly*) Oh, it's nothing personal, Walter—and now,
please go. I'm expecting my first chap any minute now.

Walter He's coming here?

Polly They're both coming here. That's what I borrowed this place for.

Walter What's this friend of your brother's going to say to your using his
pad like this?

Polly Adam Dexter? He won't know. He's away for the week-end. Otherwise I wouldn't be here. And you'd better get back to Old Daisy and
the bull before you lose your job.

Walter (*sitting down firmly*) To Hell with Old Daisy—and the job. I'm
going to stick around here and see what these computerized Romeos
have that I haven't got. So carry on—don't mind me. (*He picks up one
of Adam's girlie magazines*) Whoosh! I say! Get a load of this bird!

Polly (*snatching the magazine from Walter*) Stop leering, Walter. (*The page
gets torn*) Now you've torn her in half.

Walter I'll soon shove her together again. There—the chap won't notice.

Polly He'd be blind if he didn't. You've put her feet where her bottom
ought to be.

Walter Who cares so long as her Bristols are in the right place! (*He laughs
lecherously*)

Polly That does it, Walter! I don't know what these computerized
Romeos have to offer—and I don't care—but I'm perfectly capable of
finding a husband for myself, thank you. So will you go away and let me
get on with it.

Walter No need to shout, I know when I'm not wanted. You go ahead—
and the best of British luck to you. You're going to need it.

Walter turns smartly round, knocks over the lamp, and walks out

The lamp falls on Polly

Polly (*righting the lamp*) Hell—damn—and blast. Temper-temper, Polly,
remember, his cows love him. Oh, God, the time!

*Polly picks up her hat, goes through to the other room and throws it on the
bed in the alcove. She turns on the transistor, then switches on the electric
kettle in the kitchen. She returns to the alcove and pulls the curtains closed*

Adam Dexter enters in the corridor, carrying a zip bag

Adam Home sweet, home!

Adam pushes the sailing cap back on his head, fumbles for his key, opens the door, comes in, bangs it shut, hurls the cap off, drops his anorak on the floor, kicks his shoes off and leaves them, goes through the door, takes in the radio playing, the partly closed curtain

Hello, there, Harry old boy—it's me—Adam—I'm back. Oh, good—you've got the kettle on. (*He turns the transistor off*) And don't ask me how I got on with that blonde bird from the typists' pool because I didn't. You know what we're always saying about dumb blondes, Harry? Well, you can forget it. And I really thought I had it made this time. Hired a cabin cruiser at Cookham-on-flaming-Thames—double berth—and what a double berth! Bought this cap, two bottles of plonk, a Frank Sinatra L.P.—*Strictly for Lovers*—and I was all set to make a meal of it. And did I get it? No. She brings her Mum. Her Mum! And Shirley and her Mum settle into my double berth like two broody hens in a coop. And I'm supposed to bed down in the cockpit and have myself a ball with a punctured lilo and a wet packet of ciggies. And that's not all—Shirley's Mum starts rabbiting on about naming the day! And in case you don't know what that means—it's marriage to you, cock. And you know how I feel about marriage? Strictly for suckers. And when I talk about love. I mean a quick flick round the mulberry bush—not a mortgage like a millstone round my neck, a pram in the garage instead of a Jag—and her mother. So I said to myself —"Adam—this is where you run." And I ran my car into a bloody great ditch and had to thumb my way back on a fish lorry. There's only one place for this lot—down the laundry chute. (*He picks up his sweater and trousers, goes to the laundry chute*
Chute G-boign—g-boign—g-boign—GULP.
Adam And do I need a shower. It wasn't cheap you know, Harry. Fifty pounds for the boat; four pounds for the hat and ninety pence for the plonk.

Adam sits down on the banquette, takes his socks off, chucks them over his shoulder into the alcove. Polly chucks them straight back

Perhaps you're right, Harry. (*He puts them down the chute*)
Chute G-boign—gulp. G-boign—gulp.

The kettle whistles, Adam turns to the kitchen

Adam All right, want a cup of tea? I'm going to put a slug of whiskey in mine. Last night's little lot has shot my nerves to pieces. (*He goes into the kitchen*)

Polly tries to hook her bra off the chair with her umbrella

It just shows how careful you have to be not to get caught, Harry. Women—they're predatory little bitches.

Polly hooks the bra

And when I say bitches, Harry—I mean bitches——

Adam returns with a mug of tea

The bra drops off the umbrella, Adam notices it—picks it up

—without one single, solitary exception. (*He holds the bra up, concludes Harry has a girl there*) Er—of course, there must be exceptions—(*holding up the bra*)—pardon me, ma'am—and—er—I'm frightfully sorry, Harry—you, too, dear—I'll push off and you carry on—I mean, *I'll* carry on—take a shower and let you get on with it. Oh—I'll leave—your thing—her thing—it—here. (*He tosses it on the banquette*) Thirty-two A cup—not bad.

Adam exits to the bathroom

Polly, with the sheet draped around her sari-wise, darts out of the alcove and grabs the bra

Adam enters from the bathroom

Oh, sorry, duckie. Harry, what have you done with the towel? (*He picks up the towel, looks appraisingly at Polly*) Oh, could you ask Harry how long he'll be? No, I'd better ask him myself. Excuse me. (*He takes a step up to the alcove*) Harry, O.K. if I come back after lunch?

Silence

After tea?

Silence

After dinner?

Silence

You are going to be exhausted, Harry. (*Loudly*) Dammit, why don't you answer me, Harry?
Polly Because he's not there.
Adam Not there? You mean he's gone out?
Polly He's not been here. (*Picking up the bra*) And it's not thirty-two A cup, it's thirty-four B cup.
Adam I don't care if it's the F.A. cup. What are you doing here?
Polly Harry said I could stay here.
Adam That's cool. I said *he* could stay here—not you.
Polly (*about to empty the mug down the sink*) Have you finished your tea?
Adam No, I have not! (*Grabbing the mug*) Who are you?
Polly I'm Polly Glover.
Adam (*following her, mug in hand*) Not Harry Glover's sister?

Polly straightens the cushions on the banquette

Polly Yes.
Adam Why isn't Harry here?

Polly He didn't come. Stayed home to play rugger.

Adam Wait a bit—you must be the kid I used to see in sweater and jeans cheering Harry on from the touch-line.

Polly I am.

Adam I wouldn't have recognized you.

Polly I'm not wearing sweater and jeans.

Adam You're not wearing anything!

Polly Nor are you. How do you do?

Adam (*seizing a fur rug*) How do you do? (*They shake hands*) Er—this is a bit awkward—I mean, Harry should have let me know.

Polly But he said it would be O.K. You were holed up with this French bird at Cookham!

Adam ⎰I'm sorry—I'm not . . . ⎰*Speaking*
Polly ⎱I'm sorry too but . . . ⎱*together*

Adam ⎰So I'm afraid—you can't stay here . . . ⎰*Speaking*
Polly ⎱I'm afraid—you can't stay here . . . ⎱*together*

Adam ⎰I mean—you'll really have to go . . . ⎰*Speaking*
Polly ⎱That is—you'd really better go . . . ⎱*together*

Adam The thing is—I want to go to bed . . .

Polly You see—I've got to get dressed—this minute—I'm expecting people.

Polly looks through the glass door, sees Adam's scattered clothes

Oh lor. (*She goes through the glass door*)

Adam Expecting people? (*Following Polly*) Are you throwing a party—here—in my flat?

Polly Not a party. Just two men.

Adam And how many birds?

Polly Only me.

Adam You *are* going to be exhausted.

Polly I'm not having them both together. Just one for breakfast and one for lunch.

Adam My poor girl, this is London. These men you've invited are going to expect more than breakfast, and lunch.

Polly So do I! I expect marriage. (*She drops Adam's jacket down the laundry chute*)

Adam Marriage? Believe me—that's not what they'll be after.

Polly Believe me, it is. Otherwise they wouldn't be coming from a Marriage Bureau.

Polly takes the mug from his unresisting hand, leans over the hatch, pours his tea down the drain

Adam Marriage Bureau? What's a girl like you want with a Marriage Bureau? Aren't there any men in your part of the country?

Polly Plenty. And they all have the same idea as you—a quick flick round the mulberry bush and run like hell at the idea of naming the day— that's marriage to you, cock.

Adam Mr Dexter to you, Miss Glover. And you weren't meant to hear that.

Polly No. But from what I do hear, ninety per cent of the chaps are like you and the girls have all the wear and tear of working their way through ninety men to get to the ten who want to get married.

Adam Work their way through ninety men? That's not wear and tear—that's a career.

Polly Not *my* career, Mr Dexter. So I had the Marriage Bureau pick me two likely fellows to check over here.

Adam Not here, you don't, Miss Glover—that's for sure. Because the moment I've taken a shower, I'm going to bed. I haven't had a wink of sleep and I'm pooped.

Polly But what about my two men coming here?

Adam If either of those cowboys sets foot here I'm going to have the greatest pleasure in throwing him out.

Adam exits to the bathroom

Polly picks up her bra and panties, and goes towards the alcove

Walter enters in the corridor and rings the bell

Polly Number One—and I'm not ready! (*She hitches the sheet, goes through to the door, bends down, coos through the letter-box*) I'm terribly sorry—I seem to have overslept. Would you mind coming back a lttle later?

Walter It's me, Polly—Walter.

Polly Walter? Again! (*Shouting through the letter-box*) What do you want?

Walter My pipe. I went without it.

Polly picks his pipe up, opens the door

Polly Here you are. Run along and don't come back—I'm busy.

Walter steps forward to take the pipe, steps on Polly's trailing sheet. It unwinds as she turns away

   Walter!

Walter (*stepping back*) Oh, sorry. Hey, what on earth are you wearing?

Polly Leisure wear. Now, get lost. (*She goes through the door, into the alcove and draws the curtain*)

Walter What sort of leisure can she be busy at—in a sheet? (*Following Polly through the door*) Hey, Polly? Poll—ly . . .

Walter stops, takes in the man's dresser, picks up a battery razor, sees a man's pair of shoes, drops them when he hears Adam break out with "Down among the dead men". Walter scrambles up and peers through the transom. Walter steadies himself, leans further to look through the transom

Adam enters from the bathroom in a cloud of steam: he is wrapped in a towel. He does not see Walter, picks up his razor

Walter rubs energetically to get rid of the steam

Adam (*creeping up on Walter*) Oye!

Walter nearly overbalances, saves himself by grabbing a wall plant, holding it like a rugger ball, he manages to land with it still in his hands

Oh, well held—but don't pass it to me—I'm not playing.

Adam turns on the razor, starts shaving

Walter (*shouting above the razor*) What the hell do you think you're doing here?

Adam (*shaving unconcernedly*) Taking a shower—having a shave—going to bed. So you—out!

Walter Who do you think you are to tell me to get out?

Adam I'm Adam Dexter and I live here. (*Shaving his upper lip*) Now, buzz off!

Walter But, Polly—Miss Glover—I've got to talk to her!

Adam She's busy. I'm busy. We're both busy. Got it, cowboy?

Walter I've got it. And if it's like that, you can tell Miss Polly Glover she won't be seeing me again.

Adam (*shaving under his chin*) Great. Now, blow, cowboy—blow.

Walter (*blundering through the door*) When the Admiral hears this, he'll climb up his flagpole!

Walter exits into the corridor and off

Polly enters from the alcove, dressed

Adam Ah, Miss Glover, all tarted up for your Number One from the Marriage Bureau?

Polly Yes, Mr Dexter.

Adam Pity. I've just got rid of him. And you didn't miss much—a hairy bean-pole—stomping round in a pair of Hush-Puppies.

Polly Hush-Puppies? Oh, dear.

Adam What do you mean—"oh, dear"? The po-faced idiot was up there —leering at me in the shower! I pretty soon showed him the door. "I'm Adam Dexter", I said, "and I live here—and I'm busy". He got the message loud and clear.

Polly Message? What message?

Adam That he was intruding on you and me in our little love nest, ducky. He won't be back. So it's over and out for you, Miss Glover!

Adam laughs triumphantly. Polly laughs gaily

Polly No, it's over and out for you, Mr Dexter. That wasn't my Number One.

Adam Not? Then who was he?

Polly His name's Walter—and he works for my father—and he's off like a rocket to tell the Admiral——

Adam (*horrified*) The Admiral!

Polly —that a layabout called Adam Dexter is having it off with his darling little daughter.

Adam But I haven't and I didn't.

Polly Those are the exact words this boyfriend of my sister's said to Daddy—two weeks later, Daddy had them married.

Adam Married? You can't make a fellow get married just like that.

Polly Daddy can. He announced it in *The Times* without telling the fellow. (*Pause*) And in the Hickey column, too.

Adam Hickey? Tricky. (*Without thinking, he shaves his chest*) AIIH!!

Polly Never mind—when you meet Daddy here—with me—in that towel —you'll be able to talk your way out of it, I'm sure.

Adam Meet—Daddy?

Polly When he comes here to fetch me home, of course.

Adam (*after a pause*) Yes, of course—but I won't be here—I've just remembered. I've got a date. (*Going to the cupboard with casual speed*) Come to think of it, I'm late already—so I'll just throw on a few clothes —toddle along. (*Tugging at the cupboard door knob*) Silly—seems to have got stuck . . .

Polly It's locked. What you need is the key.

Adam (*with controlled haste*) I know what I need is my key and what I am about to get is my key out of my bag.

Polly You don't seem to trust your friends much.

Adam (*trying to unzip the bag from the wrong end*) It's not them—it's the valet—he keeps borrowing my best suits to go to all-night parties. (*He struggles with the zip*)

Polly Don't blame the zip. Zips always know when you're in a temper.

Polly takes the bag, opens it easily. Adam snatches it from her, and pulls out of the bag a woman's blouse, skirt, bra

Goodness, do you wear it for support—or is it just for kicks?

Adam I've brought the bird's bag. Now, what am I going to do for clothes? They're all locked up in that cupboard.

Polly (*holding up the blouse*) Well, drag's all the thing, isn't it? Try the dress on for size. You won't need the bra.

Adam (*snatching the clothes from Polly*) Very funny. (*He crams the clothes back in the bag*)

Polly It was only a suggestion.

Adam In very bad taste.

Polly Have you got a better one?

Adam Something's going to give and it's going to be that door.

Adam puts one hand on the door, one on the handle, gives a quick tug and steps back, and the handle comes off

That's all I needed!

Polly Keep cool, Mr Dexter.

Adam turns round, the handle in his hand, the door shut

Adam I *am* cool—cool as a flaming cucumber.

Polly goes to the house telephone

Polly I've had an idea. (*On the phone*) Hello, Porter? Look—some clothes have just been sent down the laundry chute and now we want them back. I know it's a holiday and I don't expect them to be washed. Dirty will do. Well, who has the keys to the basement? James? Well, see if he's there. (*To Adam*) Who's James?

Adam The valet. He works here—presses us gentlemen's pants—does for us—but what he likes best is passing dainty canapés at parties and arranging flowers.

Polly How very queer!

Adam Right. He's commonly known as the Nijinsky of the Service Lifts. Please, God, he's left his keys in the Service Room.

Adam exits by the Service Door

Polly Never mind the clothes, Porter! I want to order breakfast —for two. I thought these were service flats? The holiday. Kitchen's closed. But I haven't got a bite of food here! I was relying on you. O.K. Then nip along to the self-service. You've got two feet, haven't you? Ah, a wooden leg? Oh, I'm most awfully sorry, Porter. When did it happen? At Waterloo? WATERLOO! Oh, the station. No, no, don't move a step with your poor leg. I'll go myself.

Polly takes her bag and exits up the corridor.
Adam enters from the Service Door. He is wearing a pair of very tight trousers with braid down the side, a shirt, a bow-tie, and carrying a short jacket. He comes into the sitting-room and through the glass door

Adam I couldn't find his keys so I borrowed his gear. Mustn't split the old darling's pants—he's only got the one pair. (*He sits down carefully to put on his shoes*) Watch it, dearie! (*He picks up the jacket and looks at himself in the mirror*) Oh, boy, I hope I don't meet anyone I know. (*He looks at the jacket*) No, I don't think this thing will do much for me— or if it does, it will be the wrong thing.

Walter enters from the corridor and goes to the glass door

Walter sees Adam, who does not see him

(*Loudly to the closed curtain*) Well, good-bye, Miss Glover! (*Pause*) Miss Glover, I'm off!

Adam turns to go, comes face to face with Walter

Walter You're not going anywhere, matey! (*He grabs Adam by the shirt front*) Not in one piece, anyway.

Adam Wait—I can explain—all lies—just for a giggle . . .

Adam tries a feeble giggle, which develops into a gurgle as Walter shakes him

Walter I'll give you giggle! I've been talking to the porter and he says everybody knows where Adam Dexter is—*he's* holed up with a bird on the river at Cookham. So come on—let's have it!

Adam (*faintly*) Have what?

Walter (*shaking Adam*) Your name, man—your name?

Adam (*croakily*) None—of—your—business!

Walter Admiral Glover will make it *his* business!

Adam Admiral Glover! (*Looking at the jacket*) I'm—James.

Walter James? James who? James what?

Adam (*putting on the jacket*) Just James. (*Pointing to the name on the jacket*) J-A-M-E-S. Look, it's written on my left tit.

Walter (*looking Adam up and down*) What do you do here?

Adam I oblige the gentlemen in the block—sir.

Walter Doing what?

Adam I press their pants, scrape egg stains off their ties, sew on their buttons, but what I like best is arranging flowers and passing canapés at parties.

Walter The porter told me about you—you're the Pavlova of the Lifts?

Adam Nijinsky, if you don't mind, sir. And you should see the lifts. Portage is my bag.

Walter But you don't fit his description. (*Suspiciously*) Where's your ginger toupée?

Adam (*camping it desperately*) I loaned it to my friend Bas. His hair piece was at the cleaners, poor dear. It being a holiday and him being off for the week-end with the Sea Scouts, it was the least I could do.

Walter I hope he doesn't drop it overboard. Ha, ha.

Adam I'll scratch his eyes out if he does! Well, Choi.

Adam goes to exit

Walter Hold it! Why were you shaving—here?

Adam Er—I'd just mended the razor—for that nice Mr Dexter—and I was trying it out. And it's working lovely, don't you think? Smooth as a baby's bumpty-bum? Must go now. Choi.

Walter Just a minute, Pavlova—what were you doing stark naked in the shower?

Adam Stark naked in the shower? Well—glad you asked—there appeared to be more cold water than hot coming through the holes, so I was checking up that the hot water holes weren't stopped up—I could hardly do that in this uniform, sir—I've only the one, you know.

Walter (*incredulously*) You thought that in a shower hot water comes through hot water holes and cold water through cold water holes?

Adam Doesn't it, sir?

Walter My poor old darling—the hot and cold water come through the same bloody holes. That's the point of the whole flaming thing.

Adam Well, imagine that! I'll know another time and thank you, sir—ever so.

Walter How could I have thought you were Adam Dexter, my old darling?
Oh, no offence meant.

Adam None taken, I'm sure. How could I have thought you were one of
those computerized drips from the Marriage Bureau?

Walter That damned Marriage Bureau! Polly Glover should be marrying
me.

Adam You want to marry her? She's got a sucker—a fine gentleman like
you ready and willing?

Walter I'm ready and willing all right.

Adam Oh, you virile beast! And what a naughty girl Miss Polly is—playing
you up like this. If I were you, I'd take the girl by the scruff—of her neck,
chuck her in the back of the car and drive off with her.

Walter You mean—bounce her?

Adam I should wait until I get her to bed for that. But don't hang about
here—what if Mr Dexter came back.

Walter My God, he wouldn't, would he? The porter says he wouldn't
trust Adam Dexter with a three-thousand-year-old mummy!

Adam And Miss Polly's not a mummy—yet.

Polly enters in the corridor and into the apartment with a bottle of milk

Walter sees her through the glass door

Walter She's here!

Adam (*pushing Walter through the glass door*) I'll pack her bag.

Polly Are you here again, Walter?

Walter Yes. Come here.

Walter grabs Polly

Polly Look out! You'll spill the milk. What do you think you're doing?

Walter I'm taking you home. James is packing your bag.

Polly James? What are you talking about? (*She puts the milk on a table*)

*Adam enters from the alcove, carrying Polly's suitcase. It is spilling clothes
in all directions*

James? What on earth . . .

Adam (*talking non-stop*) Here we are, miss, all ready to go. If only I'd
known this nice gentleman was your fiancé, miss, and come to take
you home to Daddy, I'd never have sent him away like that—indeedy-
not. But that's silly old James all over!

Polly Silly old James?

Adam (*pointing at the name on the jacket*) Yes, miss—James. J-A-M-E-S.
And very silly, too, miss—could have got that nice Mr Dexter into
trouble with your Daddy—indeedy-yes—but luckily *everybody* knows
that Mr Dexter isn't here. So off you go, sir. (*Shaking Walter's hand*)
And can I say you're a very lucky man? (*Turning to Polly*) And may I
kiss the happy bride?

Polly You may not. I'm not his bride. Now, once and for all, Walter—
go away!

Walter But these blokes from the Marriage Bureau. You don't know a
thing about them.

Polly (*ferreting in her bag*) I do—I do! Here's Number One. And he comes
from Harrisville, Virginia. And his name is Lester B. Pearson the Second.

Walter And what does that tell you about him?

Polly He's American.

Walter Damn it all, Polly—a Yank! And who's the other one?

Polly A frog or a wog—now, push off.

Adam Well, now after that dear little lover's tiff, off you two go and kiss
and make up.

Adam hands Walter Polly's suitcase

Walter Not me!

Walter drops Polly's bag. It flies open

I'm through with you, Polly, and when the Admiral gets to hear about
this computer suitor, he'll be here at a rate of knots, firing broadsides in
all directions. And don't say I didn't warn you!

Walter goes off up the corridor

Adam For God's sake, you want a husband—why don't you save yourself
—and me—all this bother and just marry Walter?

Polly (*picking up her clothes*) Would you marry Walter?

Adam No. But I've got a good reason. I'm a man.

Polly In that dinky little suit, one might have doubts.

Adam I'll soon put your doubts to rest about that, Miss Glover. Adam
Dexter's in the clear so it's off with James and back to normal.

Polly What are you getting undressed for?

Adam Why shouldn't I? I live here. I shall go around stark naked if I
like and it won't be any of your business, Miss Glover, because you're
leaving—now.

*Lester B. Pearson—Beau—enters the corridor. He is a courteous Ameri-
can, conservatively dressed in a linen suit. He wears a panama hat and
carries a florist's box. He checks the number and rings the bell*

Polly Someone at the door!

Adam Your Number One? Great! I'll throw him out—just as I am. (*He
makes for the door*)

Polly What if it's Walter? How are you going to explain the stripping off
again?

Adam Why should it be Walter? Silly suggestion—it's always that bloody
man! (*He struggles with the zip on his pants*) This zip's stuck!

Polly I told you, zips always know when you're impatient—this time it's
your stomach in the way—pull it in.

Adam James must wear a girdle. Give me the jacket.

Beau rings the bell again

Polly Wait—your tie! Good thing it's snap-on and not do-it-yourself. (*She snaps it on roughly*)
Adam I wouldn't have called that a woman's gentle touch. (*He heads out of the alcove and through the glass door*)
Polly (*following Adam*) Hold it! Your shirt tail's sticking out. Just like a dear little bunny. I'll fix it. (*She rams the shirt down*)
Adam I'll fix my own tail, thank you, Miss Glover. (*He tucks his shirt in*)
Polly Just as you like, Mr Dexter.

Adam goes to the door and flings it open

Beau Good morning. (*Pause*) My name is Lester B. Pearson the Second. (*Pause*) Miss Polly Glover is expecting me.
Adam (*hissing angrily*) Miss Polly Glover is not at home. (*He starts to close the door*) Go away!
Polly (*quickly*) Of course I'm home. Do pull yourself together, James. Come right in, Mr Pearson.
Beau Thank you, ma'am.

Beau automatically hands Adam his hat and gloves, keeps the flowers

Thank you, son. (*Handing the florist's box to Polly*) For you, ma'am—and if I may make so bold—real English roses for a real English rose.
Adam (*wincing*) Ouch!
Polly As you're obviously not feeling well, James, you'd better go off duty —now.
Adam I will—before I have one of my nasty turns.

Adam goes into the corridor. Polly shuts the door firmly

Polly Such beautiful roses. I must go and put them in water.

Adam looks at the hat and gloves, rings the bell

Oh, excuse me. (*She gives the flowers back to Beau, opens the door. Whispers*) Will you go away! Oh, those . . . (*She snatches the hat and gloves*)
Adam I'll give you one minute flat to get rid of that corn cob before I throw him out. (*He throws himself down on the bench, lights a cigarette*)
Polly You dare! (*She slams the door*) That James! Nearly walked off with your things.
Beau Let me take them.
Polly No, no—you sit down.
Beau Thank you. (*He sits*) Coming to London, England, to get myself a wife was my grandma's idea. But around Piccadilly Circus I didn't seem to meet the kinda girl my grandma had in mind so I went to this Marriage Bureau and I guess their little old computer came up with the answer in one. Miss Polly, you surely are what we used to call down in old Virginney, a real live Honey-doll.

Polly Honey-doll? How kind of you to say that, Mr Pearson.
Beau Not Mr Pearson, please—my name is Lester Beauregard . . .
Polly The B's for Beauregard!
Beau Comes from the Louisiana branch of the family. French, you know.
All my friends call me—Beau.
Polly Beau, may I ask you something?
Adam What the hell can they be doing?

Adam opens the letter-box, listens

Polly This place you live in—Harrisville, West Virginia. What sort of a
place is it?
Beau It's real nice, Miss Polly. Right in the middle of the Blue Grass
country.
Polly Grass? Cows? Beau, you don't keep cows, do you?
Beau No. I don't rightly know if the patio is big enough, but if you should
want for us to have a cow, I'll surely find some place to corral it.
Polly No, no, Beau! No need!
Beau Miss Polly, you want a cow—you shall have a cow.
Polly But I don't want a cow!
Beau I feel you do, Miss Polly.
Polly But I don't, Beau!
Beau I got the impression you did.
Adam She doesn't want a flaming cow!
Beau Well, anything you *do* want, Honey-doll, you only have to say
because for you—I'd climb the highest mountain.
Adam With luck, he'd break his bloody neck.
Beau You should be taken care of—looked after—waited on—cherished
like a precious jewel . . . (*Taking Polly's hand*) May I—kiss your hand—
Honey-doll?

*Adam gives a piercing growl. Polly notices the flap open, takes her hand
quickly from Beau*

Polly Excuse me, one moment, please, Beau.

Polly flings the door open, knocking Adam over

Eavesdropping! How low can you sink!
Adam If you can't get rid of him, I soon will.
Polly I don't want to get rid of him.
Adam Right. Move over. You can sell anything to a Yank if you get the
image right and by the time I've finished with yours, he'll be ready to
eat his Honey-doll with a spoon. (*He pushes Polly aside and enters the
apartment*)
Beau Honey-doll, I was just thinking . . .
Adam It's me, sir—James, sir. I should not have gone off duty and left
Miss Polly alone with a gen'lman friend—suh.
Polly That'll do, James.
Adam Now, now, Miss Polly, you all knows how we is all very, very

particular about our Miss Polly's gen'lmen friends. Oh, yes, suh, Mass
Beau—suh.

Polly I think you've seen *Gone with the Wind* once too often. Pay no
attention to him, Beau.

Beau (*rising*) No, Miss Polly. (*To Adam*) I admire it in you, son, to be so
concerned about the young lady—seeing as how she's such a lovely
young lady. You seem like a regular guy.

Adam It depends what you mean by regular.

Polly (*thrusting the florist's box at Adam*) James, my flowers, please. (*To
Beau*) James just loves to arrange flowers—what he can do with a handful
of pansies and a pussy willow is out of this world!

Adam Oh—but Miss Polly can sew, knit, crochet, cook—now, Miss
Polly's home-baked apple pie is better than Mom ever made.

Polly That's quite enough of the commercial.

Adam I was only assuring the gentleman that you weren't a stranger to
gracious living, miss.

Polly Then perhaps you could show the gentleman some of this gracious
living, and serve breakfast. With a little grace?

Beau is about to sit down

Adam A little grace? Oh. (*Reverently*) "For what we are about to
receive . . ."

Beau Oh, pardon me.

Polly That'll do, James.

Adam But I haven't finished. "May the Lord make us truly thankful."

Polly Shut up, James.

Adam Still haven't finished.

Beau Amen.

Adam Thank you, sir.

Polly All right—carry on.

Adam Carry on?

Polly Yes, pull it out for him.

Adam Oh, the *chair*.

Beau That's all right. I can manage. (*He is about to sit down*)

Adam Oh, no, sir. Allow me.

*Adam whips the chair away with a flourish, Beau starts to lower himself into
space*

Polly Beau—look out!

Adam drops the chair, seizes Beau, sits in the chair with Beau on his lap

(*To Adam*) What do you think you're doing?

Adam Musical bumps, miss?

Beau Come again.

Adam It's an old English game, sir. When the music begins, we can start
all over again. Look! I'll show you, sir. (*He does*) Tra-la, round and
round we go. The music stops and down we go.

Polly Stop it, at once! Excuse me, Beau, but I'd like a word with James in the kitchen.

Polly goes through the glass door, followed by Adam

Adam Excuse me, sir.

Polly Why can't you just go away and leave me alone?

Adam But I'm doing great. Look how he lapped up that gracious living bit.

Polly He damned nearly lapped it up off the floor.

Adam I thought I fielded him rather neatly but if that's all the thanks I get—you can take old Virginney out of here—right now!

Polly But he's come to breakfast!

Adam He wants breakfast, there's a café up the road. I'll give you ten seconds flat to wheel him off. These pants are killing me! (*He goes into the alcove, draws the curtains*)

The house telephone rings, Polly answers it

Polly Hello?... Speaking... A gentleman on the phone for me?... Oh my God—Number Two—tell him to hang on. I'll be right down. (*She looks nervously at the curtain, tiptoes to the door, opens it, closes it*) Oh, Beau, I'm most awfully sorry—you'll have to excuse me just for a moment. I have to go down—have a word with—the porter.

Beau But you're coming back, Honey-doll?

Polly Just as fast as I can.

Polly goes out, banging the door, hurries along the corridor, and exits

Beau picks up the florist's box, looks round uncertainly, makes for the door. Adam opens the curtain, looks out, listens, comes out of the alcove, cautiously opens the door. Beau is hidden behind it

Adam (*going to the front door and bending down to bolt it*) Thank God, they've gone.

Beau Oh, James ...

Adam Aeih! (*Looking round*) Where is she?

Beau Miss Polly? Oh, she had to go and talk with the porter. But she'll be right back. I wondered, James—seeing as how you're a real expert on flower arrangements—maybe ...

Adam Oh, yes, I'll just go and put them in water.

Adam goes through the door, throws the flowers down the chute, and returns to Beau

Beau Thank you, James. I guess I'll be getting to know you real well.

Adam I can't think why.

Beau Visiting Miss Polly here over the next few weeks.

Adam Here? Weeks?

Beau Courting a girl takes time.

Adam You haven't got time. Just pop downstairs—now—and grab her. Where's your hat?

Beau I couldn't do that. I want to be married in church, my Honey-doll dressed all in white—and with her folks giving us their blessing.

Adam Her folks? What you'll get from that lot's a blasting—not a blessing.

Walter enters in the corridor, rings the bell

That'll be her back. (*Putting Beau's hat on his head*) Now, open the door—hold out your arms—say, "I love you"—kiss her and walk her straight down the passage and into the lift. (*Handing Beau his gloves*) Good luck.

Adam exits into the kitchen

Beau opens the door, holds out his arms

Beau Honey-doll—I love you—oh, pardon me!

Walter I've got something to say to you, Mr Lester B Pearson.

Beau You know who I am?

Walter You bet I do. Polly told me. And she's not marrying you.

Beau Oh, gosh, oh, gee—James told me how it would be. Say, why don't you sit down—and we'll talk this thing through—over a cup of coffee?

Walter There's nothing to talk through. And I'd advise you to get lost—now—before you find yourself being blasted to hell by a broadside. Get it?

Beau Sure. A blasting, not a blessing. Hold it. I'll be right back. (*He hurries through the door, and knocks on the shutter*) James, you were right about Miss Polly's folks! There's a fellow out there come to take her home—now!

Adam (*opening the shutter*) What kind of a fellow?

Beau Rugged—real rugged. He's going to blast me to hell with a broadside!

Adam A broadside! My God—the Admiral!

Adam pulls down the shutter with a thud on Beau's hat

Beau Ouch! Hey, James—open up! I want some coffee—to soften the fellow up. James—open up!

The shutter goes up just far enough for Adam to push the electric coffee-pot and lead through, closes again

What's gotten into him? (*He knocks politely on the shutter*) James?

Muffled mumblings from behind the shutter

What was that? You've picked a great time to have a nose bleed, that's all I can say. (*He carefully carries the coffee-pot through the glass door*) I guess we'll have to take care of ourselves—poor James has gotten a nose bleed.

Walter He's not the only one who's liable to get a bloody nose.

Beau Yeah—let's have ourselves a cup of coffee, huh? (*He pours into a cup*)
Walter Call that coffee? It's water.
Beau Oh, gee, I guess it hasn't perked yet.
Walter Give it to me. (*He takes the lead*) I'll plug it in. (*He goes under a table by the wall, to a switch*)
Beau (*looking nervously at loose wires in his hand*) Is this end O.K.?
Walter (*under the table*) Yes, of course. O.K.?
Beau O.K.

Walter switches on, Beau is electrified and attached to the wire gets into an animated jig

Walter Hey, steady on!

Walter puts his hand on Beau, and takes off too

Adam enters from the kitchen

Adam What the hell's going on?

Adam touches Walter. They all three take off, arms and legs gyrating

Polly enters from the corridor. She takes in the situation, kicks the switch off with her foot

Beau subsides immediately into a chair. Adam gradually stops twitching and flops on to the table. Walter continues to flay around, nearly knocking Polly down

Polly (*pushing Walter through the door*) You great clumsy oaf—get out! Get out of here! (*She shuts the door*)

Walter reels off up the corridor

Oh, Beau—Beau, are you all right?
Beau (*moaning inarticulately*) Miss Polly—James—coffee-pot . . . (*He collapses*)
Polly (*to Adam*) Don't just stand there—pick him up!
Adam Pick him up? I don't know that I can pick myself up.
Polly (*soothingly to Beau*) You're all right—lean on me.

Polly gets Beau to his feet, nearly collapsing under his weight

(*To Adam*) Help me, can't you?
Adam Move over.
Polly Careful—he's in a state of shock.
Adam I'm in a state of shock, too!
Polly We must get him to bed!
Adam Why him? *I* want to go to bed! And it's *my* bed!
Polly How selfish can you get? Take his shoes off, loosen his collar, put

two pillows under his head and wrap him in a blanket. I'll get him an aspirin.

Polly exits to the bathroom

Adam humps Beau through the door and on to the bed, bangs his legs down, pulls up the blanket and draws the curtain

Polly enters with a glass of water and an aspirin

Adam Thanks. (*Taking the aspirin and glass of water and swallowing it*) I needed that.
Polly That wasn't meant for you! It was for poor Beau.
Adam Poor Beau! He's sleeping like a baby. It's my nerves that are shot to ribbons.
Polly It serves you right! First those musical bumps—and then practical jokes with coffee-pots . . .
Adam You think *I* did that to him?
Polly Yes, I do. You've been trying to stop me finding a husband ever since I set foot here. All right—you win. I'll go and put my Number Two off—but I'll tell you what you are—you're a sick, neurotic old dog-in-the-manger!

Polly goes into the sitting-room

  Mrs Darcy enters the corridor. She is a neatly dressed, middle-aged woman, carrying Adam's bag. She looks uncertainly at the number of the apartment door

Polly opens the apartment door

Adam Me sick? Me neurotic? Me OLD? You come back here! (*He opens the bedroom door, sees Mrs Darcy in the open apartment doorway*) Oh, God—the old Mum! (*He closes the door, exits to the bathroom*)
Mrs Darcy Oh, excuse me, miss, I was looking for Mr Adam Dexter's flat but I'm not sure of the number. Do you happen to know it?
Polly I most certainly do. Come in, won't you?
Mrs Darcy Oh, thank you, how kind. I've brought Mr Dexter's bag back. He went off in such a hurry last night he took my daughter's bag by mistake. You should have seen my poor Shirl's face this morning when she opened his and found nothing but two bottles of wine, some after shave, a packet of those you-know-whats.
Polly (*startled*) Well, no—I don't exactly know—what?
Mrs Darcy Oh, you do. They're always advertising them on the telly. Ever so popular they are—with the hole in them—Polo Mints! That's it.
Polly Oh—them!
Mrs Darcy So there's my Shirl with nothing left but her nightie. Mind you,

it wasn't Mr Dexter's fault. He'd suddenly remembered he had to come home and feed his poor sick little pussy cat.

Polly His poor sick little pussy cat?

Mrs Darcy Yes, it was a shame he had to go. But that's Mr Dexter all over—kind-hearted. I mean, it's not every man who'd leave his fiancée to go and feed his cat, is it?

Polly His fiancée?

Mrs Darcy Yes, Mr Dexter and my Shirl—well, it's just a question of naming the day.

Polly You'll be lucky! If anyone gets that no good layabout to the altar, it'll be a miracle.

Mrs Darcy No good layabout? Mr Dexter? It's obvious you don't know him at all. *He's* a gentleman—through and through. So if you'll kindly tell me which is his flat, I'll say good day to you.

Polly It's right here. And you won't find him feeding his poor sick pussy cat because he hasn't got a poor sick pussy cat.

Mrs Darcy No pussy cat? What does that mean?

Polly It means he's taken your Shirl for one hell of a ride—and she's not the first and she won't be the last. He's through there—help yourself.

Polly goes out, slamming the door, and exits up the corridor

Mrs Darcy Well, I never did!

Adam enters from the bathroom and goes into the kitchen, returning with a bottle of whiskey and a glass

Mrs Darcy knocks on the apartment door. Adam, about to pour himself a drink, freezes

Mr Dexter?

Adam makes a dive for the alcove, gets under the bed, abandons the whiskey bottle beside it

Mr Dexter? (*She opens the door, looks in*) Mr Dexter, where are you? It's me—Mrs D!

Beau (*from the bed*) Snore.

Mrs Darcy So there you are! Wake up, Mr Dexter, I want to talk to you!

Beau Snore, snore.

Mrs Darcy Well, really! (*She looks round, sees Polly's umbrella, prods Beau with it*) Mr Dexter, wake up! I want to know—who's that girl?

Beau groans and gives a loud snort

I'll give you snore! (*Seeing the whiskey bottle*) You've been drinking! You and your sick cat! You've been out on the tiles—with that girl. You're a no good layabout—that's what you are! Take that! (*She gives Beau a biff with the umbrella*)

Beau Ough-gh!

Mrs Darcy Is that all you can say? Well, take that—(*biff*)—and that—
(*biff*)—and that (*biff*) . . .

Beau (*moaning*) Aieh—ooh—ugh . . .

Mrs Darcy Count yourself lucky—if I weren't a lady, I'd be giving you a
proper hiding. (*She drops the umbrella, picks up her bag and goes through
the door*)

Polly enters from the corridor

You're right—he *is* a no good layabout and you're no better, my girl·

Adam crawls out from under the bed

Polly I beg your pardon?

Adam picks up the whiskey bottle and broken umbrella

Mrs Darcy Don't try coming the innocent with me! I've just seen him—
in there—lying in bed . . .

Polly *Adam Dexter's* in the bed?

Adam closes the curtain

Mrs Darcy Yes, snoring his head off—whiskey bottle by his hand and all!
But I gave him "what-for"—and if I were your mum, you'd be getting
"what-for", too.

Adam goes to the door and opens it. Mrs Darcy disappears behind the door

Adam (*to Polly*) So you're back! Well, thanks a lot for loosing that old
tigress on me. Here's your brolly—and I didn't break it—she did.

Mrs Darcy (*appearing from behind the door and taking the umbrella from
Adam*) Over your back, my lad—and I'd do it again. Shameless, that's
what you are! You and your poor sick little pussy cat you came home to
feed! The only pussy here is this hussy.

Polly I'm not!

Mrs Darcy Oh, yes, you are!

Adam Oh, no, she isn't!

Mrs Darcy Well, if she isn't, who is she?

Adam (*after a pause*) Mrs Darcy, allow me to introduce you—this is my
sister—my little sister—Polly. She just popped in to breakfast.

Mrs Darcy Your sister? But she's been saying dreadful things about you.

Adam You know what sisters are—always knocking their brothers. (*Putting an arm round Polly*) She's mad about me really, aren't you, Sis?

Polly gives him a jab in the ribs

Ouch!

Polly Don't push your luck—brother.

Mrs Darcy Well, fancy not telling Shirl you had a lovely little sister!

Polly Fancy not telling your sister you had a lovely little Shirl?

Mrs Darcy Of course, now I see you side by side, it's obvious.

Adam Obvious? What's obvious?

Mrs Darcy You're two apples off the same tree. But you're the prettier, dear.

Adam Thank you.

Polly Not you—me. (*Inspecting Adam*) He is looking a bit peaky today— like when he was a little boy—when he got a spanking, he always got the sulkywulks.

Adam I haven't got the sulky bloody wulks!

Polly (*pulling Adam's ear*) Naughty boy to talk to Sis like that.

Mrs Darcy Oh, dear, I'm afraid it's all my fault. I hope I didn't hurt you, Mr Dexter, dear?

Adam Well, you pack quite a wallop, Mrs D., but I've got a broad back.

Mrs Darcy But what will Shirl say when I tell her what I did to you? (*Getting tearful*) She'll never forgive me!

Adam Oh, yes, she will.

Mrs Darcy Oh, no, she won't! (*Sobbing*) I'll have ruined her life.

Polly Oh, no, you won't.

Mrs Darcy Oh, yes, I will. Me hitting him like that—it's put him clean off my Shirl! Just look at his face! He hates me! (*Sobbing*) He hates me! He hates me!!

Polly (*to Adam*) Now look what you've done!

Mrs Darcy *He'll* never forgive me!

Adam Oh, yes, I will!

Mrs Darcy (*sobbing into her handkerchief*) Oh, no, you won't!

Adam (*on his knees*) Oh, yes, I will. I do! (*Patting Mrs Darcy's shoulder*) You're forgiven, Mrs D.

Mrs Darcy (*recovering fast*) Oh, well, thank you, dear. I was so afraid I'd come between you and Shirl but I should have known better—when two young people are in love, nothing can come between them. Now, let's see if I can do something for your poor bruises, dear.

Adam No, no—I'm quite happy to stay black and blue.

Mrs Darcy (*getting tearful*) Oh, dear, I do feel so badly . . .

Adam Oh, not the waterworks again, Mrs D.!

Polly He's the one who ought to feel badly—leaving you and Shirl like that—telling you he had a poor sick pussy cat to feed.

Mrs Darcy Yes, that was a naughty fib.

Adam It was more than a fib—it was a downright lie. But now I'm going to tell you the truth. And the truth is that last night when I saw you and dear Shirl together, I realized I was just not good enough for your Shirl—so I did the honourable thing—I left.

Mrs Darcy You didn't have to do that, dear.

Adam I did. I saw myself as others see me—weak—selfish—a liar— rotten, all through. Ask my sister. She knows me.

Polly Well, you do have your little weaknesses but nothing that a good little wife like Shirl couldn't put right.

Adam How can you say that, Sis? Look at me—a walking Johnny Walker. The original sponge on hollow legs—that's me. (*He totters and puts the whiskey bottle to his lips*)

Mrs Darcy (*taking the bottle from him*) You're not a hopeless case yet,

I'm sure, dear. After all, Mr Darcy was a terrible one for the beer, but he was all right after we got married and I got him on to the cocoa. Like Shirl will *you*, dear, I don't doubt.

Polly I can't wait to see him happily married to Shirl and on cocoa, Mrs D. (*To Adam*) Now, all you've got to do is name the day. How about a fortnight on Saturday?

Adam How about you shutting your cakehole?

Mrs Darcy Mr Dexter, dear, what a way to talk to your little sister!

Adam Well, there you are—that's the real me. I'm a yobo—not fit for refined company like your Shirl.

Mrs Darcy That's for Shirl to say.

Polly So why don't you go right off back to the boat with Mrs D. and ask her? If her answer's "yes", who knows, by next year Mrs D. might be Grandma D.

Mrs Darcy Oh, that would be nice, dear.

Polly And your little Sis might be Aunty Polly.

Adam (*after a pause*) You've talked me round, Sis. (*Opening the door*) Give Mrs D. her bag, Sis.

Mrs Darcy But aren't you coming too, dear?

Adam Of course—but later—when I'm dressed.

Mrs Darcy (*sitting down*) Then I'll wait for you.

Adam No—er, I've got to put on my best bib and tucker for Shirl and that takes time—and think of poor Shirl all alone on the boat.

Mrs Darcy Yes, she's only got her nightie and it's ever so cold on the boat.

Adam Cold? But there's no need for you to be cold on the boat. There's a splendid little heating system.

Mrs Darcy Well—you think of everything, dear!

Adam I do. I have to. You'll find a dear little tap right at the bottom of the boat. It's painted bright red. Got that?

Mrs Darcy Yes, dear.

Adam Just turn it to the left—as far as it will go.

Mrs Darcy And then?

Adam You wait.

Mrs Darcy And that will work it?

Adam Like a bomb. Give Mrs D. her bag, Sis.

Mrs Darcy Thank you, dear. And seeing we're all going to be one big happy family, there's something you could do that would please me very much.

Adam (*suspiciously*) What, Mrs D.?

Mrs Darcy You could call me—Mum?

Adam (*relieved*) Oh, yes—Mum. Mum all the way, every time, Mum.

Mrs Darcy (*tremulously*) Mum! You can't imagine how happy you've made me!

Adam (*hastily*) Well, tootle-oo, Mum.

Mrs Darcy Ta, ta, for now, dear.

Adam waves fondly at Mrs Darcy

Mrs Darcy waves back and exits up the corridor

Adam slams the door

Polly You may be black and blue but do they deserve a watery grave?
Adam They won't drown. The boat's tethered up against the bank—
they'll just have to pick their skirts up and wade through the mud.
Polly You certainly did a good job on the old Mum, Brother dear.
Adam Just cool, Sis—cool.
Polly If I'd been you, I'd have got cool earlier—before she walloped me.
Adam Ah, but if she hadn't found you here, she wouldn't have walloped
me at all.
Polly Yes—well, I'm sorry about that.
Adam And so you should be! First your friend Walter—then Beau—then
loosing Mrs D on me—I'm in a state of total collapse—all thanks to
you, Miss Glover.
Polly All right. I'm sorry. I'll go and will you please tell Beau—where *is*
Beau?
Adam Beau? Oh, he left.
Polly He got up—and left—without a word—for me?
Adam What would you expect him to say? Thanks for the memory?
Polly I suppose not. (*Going through the door*) I'll get my things from the
bathroom and my case from the bedroom.
Adam (*following her at speed*) No, I'll get your case. I insist.
Polly Oh, well, if you insist.

Polly exits to the bathroom

Adam whips back the curtain, pulls the pillow off Beau

Beau Oh, no—no! Not any more!

The bathroom door opens. Adam sits on the pillow, muffling Beau

Polly's head comes round the door

Polly Did you call?
Adam Er—just a nasty twinge—when I sat down.
Polly Try sitting on something soft.
Adam I am!

Polly exits

Adam leaps up, pulls Beau up, puts his arms in his jacket, pulls up his tie, etc.

Come on—time to get up!
Beau No, no. Oh, it's you, James! Am I pleased to see you! First he tries
to fry me—and then he lams the living daylights out of me . . .
Adam Shocking behaviour all round.
Beau If only you'd been here, James.

Adam How right you are! If I'd been here—(*shadow boxing*)—things would have been very different—yes, sir!

Beau I'll bet. But I haven't got your guts, James. I'm chicken, James—chicken.

Adam (*getting Beau to his feet*) Don't make a meal of it. Come on.

Beau But how can I tell Miss Polly I'm a coward?

Adam I'll tell her for you. (*He feels under the bed, comes up with two shoes*) Here are your shoes.

Beau (*taking the shoes and going through the glass door*) I guess you think I'm a spineless sardine?

Adam (*opening the apartment door*) We're all as God made us.

Beau (*stopping*) Hold it. I must put my shoes on.

Adam Put them on outside.

Beau And thanks, James—thanks for everything.

Adam All part of the service, sir.

Adam shuts the door. Beau goes and sits on the seat to put on his shoes. Adam hurries back through the glass door

Polly enters from the bathroom carrying a make-up box

(*Brightly*) All ready?

Polly Yes. I thought you were going to get my case?

Adam I was, I was. But I had a sudden rush of blood to the head. That beating the old mum gave me—I expect.

Polly Try another aspirin. They're in the bathroom.

Adam Thank you, Miss Glover.

Polly (*taking two shoes from under the bed*) *Your* shoes?

Adam Oh, yes, indeed. Thank you again—so much.

Adam exits to the bathroom

Polly puts things into her suitcase. In the corridor, Beau puts his shoes on, stands up, finds himself walking crabwise, stops, takes his right shoe off, looks at it

Beau Darn it! Where did I get two left feet from? (*He goes to the apartment door, rings the bell*)

Polly comes out of the alcove, puts her suitcase down by the make-up box, goes through the glass door, opens the apartment door

Polly Beau! You've come back!

Beau Er—um—yes. That is—I was going to kind of slide off—but—oh gee, Honey-doll—now that I'm looking at you, I have to tell you—I have rabbit's blood in my veins.

Polly Really, Beau? How did that happen?

Beau Look at me! I can't even take a beating like a man.

Polly A beating? *You* took a beating?

Beau Yeah—in there—on the bed. And I just lay there—closed my eyes

—put my head under the pillow and took it. I'm just a no good, lily-livered, yellow-bellied son of a bitch.

Polly Oh, no, you're not, Beau. But I know who is. Hadn't you better put your shoe on?

Beau I can't, I know I came here with one right foot and one left—I can't figure out how come I suddenly got two left feet.

Polly Somebody must have two right feet. Come along, Beau. (*She goes towards the bed*) Come and lie down.

Beau (*following*) Ouch! I guess I have some powerful bruises, Honey-doll.

Polly (*taking Beau to bed, taking the odd shoe from him, and drawing the curtain*) I'll see to your bruises, so you just relax. And I'm going to find your right shoe.

Beau Say maybe James knows what's happened to it.

Polly Maybe. I'd say it was a certainty.

Adam enters from the bathroom

Well, I hope the aspirin did you good?

Adam Yes. As a matter of fact, I feel so much better that I think I shall get dressed and go out.

Polly Of course. Before Mrs D. turns up again and gives you some more "what-for"—you no good lily-livered yellow-bellied son of a bitch.

Adam Miss Glover—your language.

Polly I quote.

Adam Quote who?

Polly Beau. And he'd have called you worse than that if he'd known you were cringing under the bed whilst he took your beating.

Adam No, he wouldn't—he didn't know I was cringing under the bed—because he couldn't have, because I wasn't—that's to say—he's talking rubbish. (*He moves towards Polly, walking crabwise*)

Polly Then how come you've suddenly got two right feet and Beau's in there with two left feet?

Adam He's still here?

Polly Yes. And waddling around like that you look like a paralytic penguin. Here's your shoe! Catch! (*She goes through the glass door*)

Adam You can't talk to me like that! (*He stumbles, puts on his own shoe, throws Beau's shoe into the alcove, through the glass door*) Now, then, Miss Glover—I've had more than enough of you, take your suitcase—and go!

Polly *I'm* not going. I'll call my Number Two, tell him I've changed my mind and he can come round here right away—so here—(*picking up the bag*)—take your key, open your cupboard, get dressed—and go! (*She unzips the bag, pulls out Shirl's clothes again*)

Adam That lot again!

Polly I must have given her the wrong bag! (*She bursts into laughter*)

Adam (*inarticulate with rage*) You—you—grrh! I'd like to tear you limb from limb . . .

*Polly backs away, tosses Adam the bra, which he rips in half, grunting
savagely*

Polly Bravo!
Adam Shut up—it's not funny!
Polly But it is! Don't you see? When Mrs D. finds out she's got the wrong
bag, she'll be back—and how's her dear Mr Dexter going to explain
this?

Walter enters in the corridor, carrying his bag; he rings the bell

That'll be her! I'll let her in!
Adam (*gathering up the torn clothes and the bag*) Oh, God, and Shirl's
clothes in ribbons! I've got to get rid of them! (*He goes into the alcove
and looks round for somewhere to hide the clothes*)

Polly opens the apartment door

Polly Walter! I thought I told you to go away.
Walter (*pushing past her*) Well, I'm not going. I'm staying here until you're
through with this Marriage Bureau nonsense.
Polly That may be quite a while. They've got loads of men on their books
and I'm going to go through the lot until I find one that suits. (*She goes
to the apartment door*)
Walter Hey, where are you going?
Polly To get my Number Two round here for a start.

Polly goes off up the corridor

*Walter gets busy with his pipe. Adam pulls the curtain back, grabs a cushion,
shoves it into the bag*

Beau What's going on, James?
Adam There's a dear old duck—she's always popping in—you give her
this, eh?
Beau What for?
Adam She's collecting for Oxfam. Go on.

*Adam hands Beau the bag, Beau takes it to the door. Adam gathers up
Shirl's clothes, goes to the chute*

Thank God, I can get rid of this lot once and for all.
Chute G-boign—g-boign—g-boign . . .

*Beau opens the door, sees Walter lighting his pipe, drops the bag, closes the
door*

Beau (*babbling*) James—oh, gosh, oh, gee!

Beau's legs give way and he clasps Adam round the knees

It's him—in there—that terrible fellow!

Adam For God's sake, man—leave go!
Beau But he'll murder me! What am I going to do? Help me, James!
Adam Stand up and show some guts, can't you? Think of Custer's last stand.
Beau (*staggering to his feet*) You're right, James! I must go and square up to him—alone! Stand back, James!

Beau makes a bold dramatic gesture, which unbalances Adam and knocks him straight down the chute backwards. Adam disappears, the bra catches on the edge of the chute

Adam (*off*) AiehhHH!

Beau spins round, grabs the disappearing bra, leans back and takes the strain

Beau Hold on, James—hold on! *Help!* HELP!!!

Walter comes through the door, sees Beau teetering on his heels

Hold on—hold on!
Walter (*tapping Beau on the shoulder*) Hey, you—what's up?
Beau (*turning his head and coming face to face with Walter*) Oh, gosh . . .

Beau leaves go of the bra, it whisks off down the chute

Adam (*off*) AAHHhhaa-ii . . .

CURTAIN

ACT II

The same. A few minutes later.

James enters from the Service Door. He wears gay off-duty clothes, a carefully arranged gingery toupée which doesn't quite match his own salt-and-
pepperish fringe of hair. He has a jaunty step. James chooses his pass-key
off his key-ring, opens the apartment door, closes it, passes confidently
through the glass door, goes straight to the cupboard, notices the missing
door knob.*

James Now what's Mr Dexter been up to? So masterful! (*He opens the
cupboard*) Now then what'll it be today? Not the green—and I wore the
blue last time. And not the bird's-eye check either—everybody said it
made me look liverish. I haven't tried the *café au lait* yet—fabulous
colour. Be just right with my new wiggie, too. (*Looking through shirts*)
About time we got some new shirts though. This button-down bit's right
out, and not a see through among them. Still, this'll have to do for now.
And his ties! If I had the buying of them, he'd look a different girl
altogether. (*He takes the suit, shirt and tie*)

James exits through the Service Door. Adam enters down the corridor

Adam That was one hell of a bad trip. (*He pours a whiskey, goes through
the glass door, begins to take off his jacket*)

Polly enters from the corridor

Polly Adam! What do you think you're doing, I leave the place for two
seconds and you start stripping off again.
Adam Two seconds? It's been a lifetime to me.
Polly That blasted telephone—I hadn't got any change, and the porter had
disappeared because some half-wit had fallen down the laundry chute.
He must have been blind drunk, because then he managed to fall into
the garbage pit——

Adam turns

—and then . . . (*She sees and smells Adam*) Oh, no!

Adam Yes, Miss Glover——me!
Polly But you could have broken your neck! And stop drinking you've
obviously had quite enough.
Adam I haven't had a drop yet—I was tipped down the chute—by your
friend Beau.
Polly Beau? He'd never do a thing like that!

Adam His legs turn to jelly at the sight of Walter and he wraps himself around the nearest thing like a dying octopus—the nearest thing was me—AND I END UP SMELLING LIKE A LOAD OF . . .

The house telephone buzzes

Exactly!

Polly (*answering the phone*) Yes, Porter, speaking . . . I'll be right down. Tell him to hold on. (*She hangs up*) I must go.

Adam grabs her wrist

Don't you understand—he's on the line—my Number Two.

Adam I don't give a fish's tit for your Number Two. I've had enough, Miss Glover. With your Number One, I joined the boys in the band and whatever's in store with your Number Two, I'm not doing it.

Polly (*prevaricating*) Er, yes—all right. I'll put him off.

Adam That's better, Miss Glover.

Polly But if you don't let me go, I'll miss him and he'll turn up here and you don't want that, do you?

Adam No, go on. (*Bundling Polly across to the front door*) Hurry up! What are you hanging about for?

Polly You'd better take a bath. There's some bath essence in the bathroom.

Polly exits up the corridor

Adam What the hell do I want with bath essence? I need a good strong sheep dip. (*He picks a piece of orange peel, from his shirt, catches sight of himself in the mirror*) That can't be me! To think that only yesterday I was a perfectly normal randy bloke—and look at me now. Not even the lowest goat-girl in the filthiest hovel in Kurdestan would drop her yashmak for me.

Beau enters, goes straight to the chute and calls down

Beau Oh, gosh—where can that fellow be, he must have got stuck in the chute—he's not at the other end. (*He calls down*) Hey, there! James! James, can you hear me? Yoo-hoo!

Adam Yoo-hoo!

Beau He's there!

Adam Not there, you fool—here!

Beau Oh, gosh—James? Am I pleased to see you! And it was all my fault! I've been looking all over for you. How d'you get here?

Adam By way of the garbage pit.

Beau (*sniffing*) Holy Mackerel!

Adam You're right. (*Picking off a fish head*) It's definitely mackerel—but certainly not holy. (*Going to the chute*) Why can't they put their fish heads down the lavvy and flush.

Chute G-boign. G-boign. G-boign.

Beau I guess I'd better go and tell them you're O.K., James.

Adam O.K.? If I were a house I'd be condemned as a slum and demolished!
Beau Not you, James. You know something? You're the toughest fairy
I ever met. (*He goes towards the apartment door*)
Adam Lifebuoy, this is your greatest test.

*Adam exits to the bathroom. Mrs Darcy enters in the corridor with
Adam's bag and rings the bell*

Beau opens the door

Beau Well, howdy, ma'am.
Mrs Darcy Oh, excuse me, I just popped back—to get my bag.
Beau You must be the dear old duck—pardon me, the lady from the Oxo
family. I guess this is your bag, Mrs Oxo, ma'am?
Mrs Darcy Mrs Oxo? I'm Mrs Darcy.
Beau Oh, pardon me again—he said you'd be popping in for this bag, so
I thought...
Mrs Darcy That's right, thank you. It's my daughter's bag, really. His
fiancée, you know.
Beau (*incredulously*) His fiancée? That guy's getting married? To a girl?
Mrs Darcy Oh, yes, to my Shirley. They'll make a lovely couple.
Beau Well, my congratulations, ma'am—and to him, too. Some fellows
surely seem to get the best of both worlds.

*Beau exits up the corridor. Adam comes out of the bathroom, finds his
empty glass, goes to get the whiskey bottle. His hair is still all over his
face, his shirt unbuttoned, his shirt tails flapping*

Adam Oh, my God, how did you get here?
Mrs Darcy On a number nine bus, Mr Dexter dear. Your little sister gave
me the wrong bag but I've got the right one now.
Adam Great. Now, you go and get back on a number nine and give Shirl
my fondest love. (*He opens the door, his leg gives way*)
Mrs Darcy What's the matter, dear? You don't look at all well?
Adam I'm perfectly all right. Just had a nasty fall.
Mrs Darcy You've been at the bottle again!
Adam I haven't, but it's not for want of trying. (*He picks up the bottle*)
Now, don't keep Shirl waiting any longer.
Mrs Darcy I'm not going to leave you in this state. (*Taking the bottle from
Adam*) You don't need any more of that. What you need is a nice cup of
tea. Where's your little sister?
Adam My little what? Oh, her! She's out. And I don't want a nice cup of
tea.
Mrs Darcy Oh yes, you, do.
Adam Oh no, I don't!
Mrs Darcy Oh yes, you do and what's more, I'm going to make it.

*Mrs Darcy goes through the door into the kitchen, puts on the kettle, and
returns*

Adam (*following her, shouting*) I don't want a cup of tea! I want a flaming drink and a flaming drink I'm going to have!

Mrs Darcy Oh, dear, I went through all this with Mr Darcy before I got him on to cocoa. First the nasty rough talk, then he'd go all tearful and then feel icky-boo. Are you feeling icky-boo yet, dear?

Adam No, I am not. Why should I? The only drink I've had today was a small tot with my morning tea.

Mrs Darcy At it first thing! Just like Mr Darcy—he'd end up reeling around with his hair all over his face, showing his chest to everyone and his shirt tails flapping.

Adam (*pushing his hair back and buttoning his shirt, crooked*) Now, look, Mrs D., I told you—I had a fall. Down a laundry chute—into a garbage pit—a nightmare—there I was in a sea of orange peel—and tea-leaves (*brushing them off himself*)—horrid little black things—look—they're all over me—ugh!

Mrs Darcy (*peering at him*) I don't see them, dear.

Adam Of course, you don't—they're on the floor now. And then there was this fish . . .

Mrs Darcy Fish, dear?

Adam Yes—here in my shirt—a skeleton—all white bones—and an eye— I took it—and threw it away—ich!

Mrs Darcy (*humouring him*) Never mind, dear. Mr Darcy used to see little green caterpillars all over him—and he once thought he had a live ferret up his trouser leg—kept dancing about and yelling at me to grab it! Oh, he did get it badly. (*Taking the whiskey bottle to the kitchen*) Best place for this is down the sink (*She returns*)

Adam (*turning round*) Best place for what?

Mrs Darcy The whiskey, dear. There—that's the last of it.

Adam You haven't—you couldn't have—not all that good booze down the drain?

Mrs Darcy Only removing temptation from you. You said yourself you had a weakness for it and you certainly have.

Adam (*practically sobbing with frustration*) Mrs D., I am not drunk! I am stone cold sober.

Mrs Darcy That's just what Mr Darcy used to say.

Adam sags wearily

Why don't you sit down, there's a good boy? (*She moves a chair*) You'll feel better when you've had your tea.

Mrs Darcy exits to the kitchen

Adam lowers himself into the space where the chair used to be, and ends up in a heap on the floor

Adam Oh God, what have I done to deserve this?

Mrs Darcy returns from the kitchen

Mrs Darcy (*seeing Adam on the floor*) Oh, Mr Dexter, dear—you're not sitting on the chair, you know—you're sitting on the floor.

Adam I know I'm sitting on the floor. When the chairs start moving about the room, I'm bound to end up sitting on the floor. (*He beats his fist on the floor*)

Mrs Darcy Oh, my goodness, he'll be eating the carpet in a minute. Here, dear—let me help you up.

Adam No, just leave me alone! (*Pathetically*) For pity's sake, Mrs D., just go away and leave me alone!

Mrs Darcy Oh, dear, here come the tears—just like Mr Darcy. Have my hanky, Mr Dexter dear?

Adam I don't want a hanky! Oh, God, I think I'm going mad.

Mrs Darcy You're all right. Just had a drop too much.

Adam Will you please listen to me, Mrs D. . . .

Mrs Darcy It's not Mrs D.—it's Mum, dear. Remember?

Adam Yes, Mum—I mean, no, Mum. It can't be Mum because I'm not marrying Shirl—I'm not marrying anyone. There, now you know.

Mrs Darcy Nonsense! That's only Demon Drink talking. You'll have forgotten you said that when you've sobered up. Where do you keep your tea-set? (*Going towards the laundry chute*) In this cupboard?

Adam Not there, for God's sake! And I haven't got a tea-set.

Mrs Darcy Fancy! Well, that's what I'll give you and Shirl for a wedding present.

Adam You can't have wedding presents without a wedding!

Mrs Darcy You're quite right, so the sooner you name the day, the sooner you'll have a tea-set. How about a fortnight on Saturday, like your little sister suggested? We know it would suit her anyway.

Adam Never mind her—what about me? I've got a very tight schedule, you know.

Mrs Darcy So has the Congregational Church in Tooting, but I happen to know it's free that day.

The kettle whistles

I'll make the tea. (*Going to the kitchen*) So that's settled—a fortnight on Saturday—unless there's a hitch, of course.

Adam (*hopefully*) What sort of a hitch?

Mrs Darcy Well, say illness. Or an accident in the family.

Adam Accident?

Adam looks at Mrs Darcy busy in the kitchen, looks at the laundry chute. He goes to the chute, thoughtfully pushes the flap back and forward an inch or two, looks again at Mrs Darcy in the kitchen. With his back to the chute, he takes one stride forward, makes his "mark" with his heel on the spot

Mrs Darcy looks out of the kitchen and sees what seem to be Adam's drunken lurchings. She comes anxiously out of the kitchen

Oblivious to Mrs Darcy, Adam steps back from the "mark" he has made, advances on the chute, hands held low as though about to heave something heavy down it. Not quite satisfied, he starts to practise again, stops when he sees Mrs Darcy

Mrs Darcy Well, I never! Mr Darcy never got it as bad as that. The sooner I get a cup of tea into you, the better. Where's the tea strainer, dear?
Adam In the kitch—er, in that cupboard. (*He points at the laundry chute*)
Mrs Darcy (*going towards it*) In this cupboard?
Adam (*following her*) Yes—Mum.
Mrs Darcy Funny sort of door. Where's the handle?
Adam It's the latest thing, Mum. It's a—push door.
Mrs Darcy A push door, dear?
Adam You push and it does the rest.
Mrs Darcy And it works, dear?
Adam Like a bomb.

Mrs Darcy goes right up to the chute, Adam right behind her

Only thing, it's a bit dark—you'll have to feel around.
Mrs Darcy Is it on the top shelf?
Adam No, on the bottom. You'll have to bend down and lean well in. Think you can manage?
Mrs Darcy Of course, I can manage. I haven't got one foot in the grave yet, you know.
Adam Not far off it!

Mrs Darcy puts her hand on the laundry chute, leans forward. Adam puts out his hand and takes a step towards her, Mrs Darcy turns round and bumps into him

Mrs Darcy Silly me! We don't need a strainer.
Adam Oh, yes, we do.
Mrs Darcy Oh, no, we don't! It's tea bags. You don't need a strainer with tea bags.

Mrs Darcy goes back to the kitchen and gets busy with the tea

Utterly dejected, Adam slumps into a chair

Adam Bloody tea bags!
Mrs Darcy (*from the kitchen*) It's more like a rabbit hutch in here than a kitchen.
Adam (*after a pause*) Oh, you're right, Mum—no good at all for Shirl. And I'd never find a place good enough for Shirl in a fortnight so there's nothing for it—we'll have to put the whole thing off while I start looking —and that could take weeks—if not months—if not years.
Mrs Darcy (*coming and going with the teapot and mugs of tea*) There'll be no need for that, dear. Shirl's got her eye on a lovely little house just across the road from me at Tooting. All mod cons—mind you, there's no garage but there's a nice shed just right for the pram. And only one

per cent down and thirty-five years to pay off the mortgage. Think of that, dear. (*She takes the teapot back to the kitchen*)

Adam The pram! The mortgage! Thirty-five years on the treadmill! Oh, God, will nobody rid me of this turbulent old bitch? (*He groans and puts his head in his hands*)

Mrs Darcy (*returning; sympathetically*) Head going round and round now, is it? Never mind—drink up your tea. Although I say it myself, I make a lovely cup of tea and I always have one myself about this time with a nice cake.

Adam Yes, yes—yak, yak—did you say—cake?

Mrs Darcy Yes, but I don't expect you've got the kind I like.

Adam Try me. What kind do you like!

Mrs Darcy Those cup cakes with sponge on the bottom, then marzipan and chocolate walnut whip and a cherry on top. They're my favourites.

Adam Well, isn't that fantastic? I've got that very thing!

Mrs Darcy You haven't, dear!

Adam Oh, yes, I have! Right there. (*He points to the chute*)

Mrs Darcy In that cupboard?

Adam Yes, Mum. Help yourself, Mum.

Mrs Darcy goes to the chute; Adam follows her

Mrs Darcy We'll I don't mind if I do. Of course, I shouldn't go nibbling between meals but there—I always say—you only live once. (*She puts her hand on the chute*)

Adam (*breathing down her neck*) That's right, Mum—enjoy life when you can. Never know when it'll be too late, eh?

Mrs Darcy (*taking her hand off the chute*) Come to think of it, I'd better not—it'll spoil my dinner. (*Turning round, right up against Adam, sniffing*) And you really ought to put on a clean shirt, dear.

Adam I haven't got a clean shirt.

Mrs Darcy No clean shirt? It's high time you had a little wife to look after you. And you want to take a bath, dear—you really do.

Adam I don't want a bath!

Mrs Darcy You may not want a bath but you certainly need one. Now, let's get that dirty shirt off for a start. (*She reaches out to Adam*)

Adam (*backing away*) Oh, no, you don't!

Mrs Darcy (*advancing on Adam*) Oh, yes, I do!

Adam Oh, no, you don't! (*He backs into the chute and the shutter opens*) Aieh! (*Clutching at Mrs Darcy*) Help! (*On his knees*) Help!

Mrs Darcy Whatever's the matter, dear?

Adam Not again! Orange peel—tea-leaves—that fish!

Mrs Darcy Oh dear, and I thought we were on the mend. Mr Darcy never went on at me like this.

Adam Mr Darcy never went through what I'm going through.

Mrs Darcy Try and get up, dear.

Adam Why should I? I've got farther to fall.

Mrs Darcy Mr Darcy once spent a whole week-end crawling about on his hands and knees—he thought he was a dog. The neighbours complained about the barking. So let's get you to bed.

Adam (*crawling to the alcove*) I'll get myself to bed.

Mrs Darcy And I'd better get Mr Darcy's doctor. He used to dry Mr Darcy out something wonderful.

Adam I don't want drying out by Mr Darcy's bloody doctor.

Mrs Darcy Then I'll get your own doctor. Where's the telephone?

Adam (*thankfully*) Downstairs.

Mrs Darcy What's your doctor's name?

Adam Er—Watson.

Mrs Darcy Telephone number?

Adam In the book.

Mrs Darcy Where does he live?

Adam In Baker Street—with his partner Holmes. (*He lies back on the bed*)

Mrs Darcy That's right, dear—you lie still and if the room starts spinning round, just hold tight to the bed. (*She closes the curtains and goes through the door*) Poor boy, he is in a bad way.

Walter enters in the corridor and rings the bell

Mrs Darcy opens the door

Walter Oh, hello? Who are you?

Mrs Darcy Mrs Darcy. Did you want something?

Walter Yes. Where's Polly?

Mrs Darcy She's out. And I'm just going to call the doctor.

Walter Wait a minute—who wants the doctor?

Mrs Darcy Mr Dexter, of course.

Walter Adam Dexter?

Mrs Darcy Yes. He's not been himself all day and now he's been taken really bad.

Walter All day? But he isn't here. He's away. (*Confidentially*) He was holed up with a fancy bird on his boat last night, you know.

Mrs Darcy He most certainly was not!

Walter Oh, yes, he was!

Mrs Darcy Oh, no, he wasn't!

Walter How do you know?

Mrs Darcy Because I was on his boat last night.

Walter Good grief, you're the bird!

Mrs Darcy How dare you? I'm no bird and nor is my daughter. My Shirl and Mr Dexter are engaged to be married. And the only place he was holed up last night was here—in his own bed.

Walter But that's impossible. Polly was here last night.

Mrs Darcy Of course she wasn't. His little sister Polly only popped in for breakfast this morning.

Walter Polly? She's not his sister!

Mrs Darcy How do you know?

Walter Because Polly Glover's my girl friend! And—if she was here—and he was here—he's no longer your Shirl's fiancé, is he? Ha, ha.

Mrs Darcy But if he was here—and she was here—she's no longer your girl friend, is she?

Walter (*stopping laughing abruptly*) That swine, Adam Dexter! Just wait until I lay my hands on him.

Mrs Darcy That's right. You give him you know what.

Walter No—what?

Mrs Darcy What-for, that's what. (*Picking up her own bag*) You'll find him lying in bed. (*Handing Walter the broken umbrella*) Here's more strength to your arm—and put a bit of beef in it—from me and my Shirl.

Mrs Darcy exits up the corridor with her bag

Walter goes to the alcove and, brandishing the umbrella, whips back the curtain

Walter All right, you—on your feet and take your thrashing like a man.

Adam Pardon?

Walter Oh, it's you, James.

Adam Of course, it's me, James. Who did you think it was?

Walter Adam Dexter, of course.

Adam What's the poor bleeder done now?

Walter It's not what he's done now—it's what he did last night.

Adam Last night? But everybody knows he was holed up with a bird at Cookham.

Walter He was not. I've just had it from the bird's mum—in there! He was here—with Polly! And when I get my hands on that stinking, rotten bastard . . .

Adam Stinking—rotten, yes—but bastard . . . ?

Walter You've been double-crossing me, James. Now, come on—*where is he?*

Adam He just left!

Walter How could he have with me here?

Adam Came out of the bathroom—said "chaio"—and went.

Walter When was that?

Adam Just now—when you were calling him a stinking, rotten bastard, sir.

Walter Why didn't you tell me?

Adam I didn't think he'd care to meet you, sir.

Walter All right. Where's he gone?

Adam South America.

Walter (*heading for the door*) He can't have got far yet. And so help me, James, if you're lying to me, I'll come back and do you! (*He goes into the corridor*)

Adam You're welcome, I'm sure.

Adam shuts the door, picks up the empty whiskey bottle, shakes it, puts it to his lips, tries to get the last dregs, exits to the bathroom

In the corridor, Walter trips on his shoelace, stops to fasten it

James enters from the Service Door, opens the apartment door with his key

Walter sees him out of the corner of his eye, looks round the apartment door. James goes to the cupboard, replaces a tie, takes another

James Better, not perfect but better. Not what I'd have chosen myself, it's too bad he doesn't have better taste in ties. Oh, well, you can't have it all ways, though it can be fun trying. (*He goes to the sitting-room*) I hope we haven't run out of fags again. (*He empties the cigarette box*) I must say I really do something for this suit—make it look quite distinguished. Lovely—that's me.

Adam enters from the bathroom

Adam I'll give him common!

Adam opens the glass door as Walter opens the front door

Walter⎱ *Hey, you!* ⎱ *Speaking*
Adam ⎰   ⎰ *together*
James Oh, goodness—oh, my goodness gracious!
Walter (*seizing James*) Got you! Adam Dexter. (*To Adam*) And you said he'd gone to South America!
Adam He missed the boat!
Walter Now look, Dexter . . . !
James Oh, no, sir—no, sir, not me, sir.
Adam Oh, goodness gracious me! Mr Dexter, sir, let me introduce you—this is Mr Walter, Mr Walter, please put Mr Dexter down, sir.
James But I'm not Mr Dexter!
Adam Now, now, Mr Dexter, sir. Let us not confuse the gentleman. Mr Walter knows I'm James and me being James, I know you're Mr Dexter, Mr Dexter.
James No, no, no—I'm not!
Adam Isn't that Mr Dexter's suit you're wearing?
Walter We'll soon see about that. (*He looks at the tailor's label of James's coat*) A Dexter, Esquire.
Adam You see, Mr Dexter—no use to deny it. (*To Walter*) Many's the time I've scraped the eggy off that tie—one of Mr Dexter's favourites, isn't it?
James If this is one of your games, I don't want to play! (*He sees his own uniform*) Hey!
Adam Ah, you're wondering what I'm doing here in your apartment dressed—or rather, undressed. Well, truth to tell, we had a little accident with our uniform—and as we've only got the one . . .

Walter Cut the cackle, James. (*To James*) Now, Admiral Glover wants to know what are your intentions towards his daughter, Polly Glover.

James Intentions? Oh, my God! The idea!

Adam He wants to know if you're going to marry Miss Glover or not, sir.

James Me? You must be mad!

Adam That's what I thought he'd say.

James Whatever next!

Walter What do you mean—whatever next?

Adam I think he means no—don't you?

James Yes, I mean—no, no, no, a thousand times no. (*He stamps his foot*)

Walter You swine—you sex-mad layabout. You're going to find yourself going up the aisle with the Admiral's six-inch gun up your backside. You don't do a thing like this to a girl like Polly and get away with it!

James But I don't know what I have done!

Adam This gentleman's under the impression you were here last night— with Miss Polly Glover, Mr Dexter.

James No, never—how could I—I was at a party.

Walter A party? All night?

Adam He's always going to these all-night parties, sauce box.

Walter So that's why you left your other bird at Cookham—to go to an all-night orgy?

Adam Hold up, Mr Dexter, sir, he's flogged flat and no wonder. You sit down, sir, and James will get you a nice little drinkie!

James Oh, no, no. I can't stop. I've got to go. I've got a date.

Walter What? Another date? Now! After last night?

Adam Got a lot more stamina than you think—our Mr Dexter. You run along, sir—and have a lovely lovely time.

James exits

Walter That bloke really is Mr Dexter, James?

Adam Tailor's tab on his suit—good as a passport!

Walter My God, he's certainly not what I'd have called a heart throb!

Adam That's the sort that's all the go these days. Well, I won't keep you.

Walter Keep me?

Adam The sooner you tell the Admiral that Mr Dexter never laid a finger on Miss Polly the better for all concerned.

Walter You're right. Where is Miss Polly?

Adam Downstairs—on the telephone. You'll catch her there if you're quick.

Walter Thanks, James—and, James, let me be your best friend and tell you—you stink!

Polly enters the corridor

Adam Really, sir? Thank you for putting it so tactfully. I'll have to get busy with the bath essence. It's Badedas.

Adam goes into the bathroom

Walter meets Polly coming into the apartment

Walter Hi, Polly!

Polly What are you doing here?

Walter Just had a chat with Adam Dexter.

Polly Adam? You've seen him?

Walter I have!

Polly Oh, my goodness. Now you listen to me, Walter—however odd it may all look to you—there was nothing—absolutely nothing between me and Adam Dexter.

Walter Oh, I know that. He made his feeling about you perfectly clear.

Polly How clear?

Walter Well: "No, no, a thousand times no." (*He stamps his foot*) You can't get much clearer than that. He's got all the birds he can handle without you, old girl. I've never seen a chap so pooped. I don't know how he gets away with it!

Polly Nor do I!

Walter Well, buck up, old girl. (*He slaps Polly's back*) Get your suitcases and we'll go.

Polly What makes you think I'm going anywhere with you?

Walter I said I'd marry you and I won't go back on my word, so you'll just have to make the best of it, because you're nowhere near getting a husband here, are you?

Polly That's what you think, Walter. I've just been on the phone to a charming man called Mr de Souza.

Walter De Souza! Sounds like a white slaver from South America.

Polly He's a widower from South Kensington. He's got three small children and he's from the Marriage Bureau, and now go away because I'm not opening the door again today to anyone except Mr de Souza.

She pushes Walter out

Walter (*in the corridor*) Three little de Souzas? The Admiral will never stand for that!

Walter exits down the corridor

Polly (*returning to the apartment*) I'll give him no, no, a thousand times no!

Adam enters from the bathroom

Adam Fantastic! Ah, Miss Glover, haven't I come up smelling like roses?

Polly No, Mr Dexter, you have not! Did you have to tell Walter quite so clearly how you felt about me?

Adam Me tell Walter? Never!

Polly You said: "No, no, a thousand times no." (*She stamps her foot*) It makes me feel as though I had the plague.

Adam Oh, not the plague, Miss Glover. Believe me, if you didn't have this fixation about marriage I wouldn't be pussy-footing around you like a celibate monk—I don't usually pass up a dishy bird when I fancy her. (*He exits to the bathroom, returns with the clothes*) And as you're such a dab hand with zips—open my bag and get out the key, there's a love. I'm going to need some really sharp gear to make out at Battersea Fun Fair.

Polly Battersea Fun Fair?

Adam Yes. In the tunnel of love you get to the basics without wasting time on the chatting up. (*He drops the clothes down the chute*)

Polly pulls out Walter's pyjamas from the bag

Chute G-boign—g-boign—g-boign.

Polly Those colours look vaguely familiar!

Adam Got the key?

Polly There's no key—just pyjamas. Will they be casual enough?

Adam Dear God, they're not mine! (*He sees the bag*) It's not my bag!

Polly It must be Walter's—it's the rugger club colours.

Adam Blimey, when the whole team's wearing these passion killers, the sex life in your part of the country must come to a grinding halt!

Polly That's the whole idea, keeps the side in training. They wouldn't do for the tunnel of love?

Adam No, they're only fit to go to bed in—alone. Which is what I'm going to do.

Polly But you can't! My Number Two will be coming!

Adam But you went down to put him off!

Polly (*happily*) We got cut off.

Adam Right, Miss Glover. I'm not having your Number Two in here, so I'll give you two minutes to collect your traps and get out.

Adam exits to the bathroom with Walter's pyjamas

Polly finds the door handle, realizes the cupboard will open, hides the handle in her handbag

Adam returns from the bathroom wearing Walter's pyjamas

All set to leave, Miss Glover?

Polly Oh, yes, er—thank you. Just got to fix my hair—won't be long.

Polly exits to the bathroom

Adam goes through the glass door to the cigarette box

Adam Damn! The old fag's had all my fags. I wonder if she's got one? (*He goes back through the glass door to Polly's bag, looks for fags but finds the door handle, opens the cupboard, puts the handle into his pyjama*

pocket) Well, well, well, well, well, well. Now that's the kind of game
I like, the sort that two can play. The sort of game I usually win.

James enters the apartment with a bag

Adam looks through the glass door and goes through

Now look here, James . . .

James Mr Dexter, dear—I'm so sorry! I don't know what came over me.
I must have come all over queer! I've never had one of your suits before,
sir—and I always give everything a good sponge and press and put it
back as good as new.

Adam But it was new. I haven't even worn it myself yet.

James And I'm sure you'll look fantastic in it, Mr Dexter, sir. You can
put it on right now and give it a quick pass in the King's Road.

Adam I don't have to go shopping in the King's Road today. I think I've
got the goods laid on right here. So you can keep that suit for today.
I don't need clothes right now.

James Oh well, if you're going to be otherwise occupied, your lady friend
won't want her clothes either.

Adam What clothes?

James (*opening the bag*) The porter told me to bring them up. (*He pulls
out the torn bra*)

Adam James, are you trying to be funny? Take it away!

James What would I do with it?

Adam Mend it!

James Oh, Mr Dexter, sir—you will have your little joke.

Adam I'm not joking! And where are my cigarettes you nicked?

James Not nicked, Mr Dexter, sir—borrowed. I'll pop out and get you
a pack. (*He holds out his hand*) Oh—I'll put it on the slate. (*He holds the
cups of the bra to his ears*) Oh! I can hear the sea!

Adam goes through the glass door

Polly enters from the bathroom

Polly Right. I'm all ready then.

Adam Miss Glover, relax!

Polly I thought I only had two minutes to get out?

Adam I've been thinking. I *have* been a neurotic old dog-in-the-manger.
You want a husband, why shouldn't you have one? And this Number
Two is your last chance so I want everything to go absolutely right
for you this time. If only I could get into my cupboard I'd get some
clothes and be able to go, wouldn't I? And then I wouldn't be here to
embarrass you? Would I?

Polly You're not embarrassing me, Mr Dexter.

Adam Oh, good. Then you won't mind if I go to bed? It may be hours
before this Number Two turns up, so we might as well fill in the time,
mightn't we?

Polly Doing what?

Adam Well, we could have a little drinkie—and play the record player—and then have another little drinkie . . .

Polly No, thank you, I'm not here to have any little drinkies.

Adam Of course. I keep forgetting. It really is a pity you're so dead set on marriage.

Polly You've said that before.

Adam It shows it's on my mind, ducky. Ooh, these pyjamas scratch! Would you mind if I took them off?

Polly Yes, I would.

Adam But, Miss Glover, you've been seeing me in the altogether ever since we met!

Polly Not altogether in the altogether.

Adam What's the matter? You've gone all nervous, ducky. I can't think why, I look like one of those cuddly teddy bears little girls take to bed with them.

Polly I'm not a little girl so this teddy bear will have to go to bed alone.

Adam Just as you like. Oh, and by the way, if I snore—the only way to stop me is to wake me with a gentle kiss—you know like the sleeping beauty?

Polly She was the princess and as for the beauty . . .

Adam (*going into the bedroom and closing the curtains*) Don't say it! I'm the beast.

Polly (*discovering the door knob is missing*) I'm sure I put it there!

Adam (*looking through*) Looking for something.?

Polly Er—no—nothing!

Adam Then let me help you look for nothing. (*On his knees*) Now, what sort of a nothing is it we're looking for? Is it a little nothing or a big nothing. (*He puts his hand around Polly's waist*)

Polly Whatever it is, Mr Dexter, you won't find it there, I shall go and wait for Mr de Souza downstairs.

Adam De Souza?

Polly Yes, my Number Two, and if he does come up here, you can tell him I'll be sitting on the bench by the telephone-box downstairs.

Adam But you can't go just like that.

Polly Why not?

Adam Er . . . (*He opens the glass door and sees James*) Because he's here.

Polly Who's here?

Adam Your Mr de Souza.

Polly Here? Where?

Adam In there.

Polly Why didn't you say so before?

Adam I didn't connect—the name De Souza and your Number Two. Come along—mustn't let him escape.

Polly No, no—I can't.

Adam Ah! Finally gone off the Marriage Jag.

Polly Certainly not!

Adam Then come on. (*Through the door*) Ah, Mr de Souza!

James What?

Adam Sorry to keep you waiting, Mr de Souza. Miss Glover, may I introduce you to Mr de Souza? Mr de Souza—Miss Polly Glover.

James Please—I must protest.

Adam Of course you must. I shouldn't be entertaining you and Miss Glover in these pyjamas. It's most embarrassing but Miss Glover'll explain to you why I haven't got a thing to wear, won't you, Miss Glover?

Polly I—don't think Mr de Souza would be interested.

James Oh! Jiminy Cricket! (*He tries to escape, but is pulled back firmly by Adam*)

Adam But that's not all! You and Miss Glover have a great deal to say to each other, Mr de Souza. I'm sure she wants to know all about you and you want to know all about her before you plunge headlong into holy matrimony.

James Holy what?

Adam Getting spliced, Mr de Souza.

James Oh, Gawd!

James collapses and is helped to a chair by Adam

Adam That was the idea, wasn't it? (*To Polly*) He's forgotten what he's come for! Have a cigarette?

James Oh, no, no.

James tries to rise but is pushed back by Adam and a cigarette shoved in to his mouth

Adam But I insist, Mr de Souza! Don't tell me you don't smoke? Now what about a drink?

James Oh, yes, sir. Right away, sir.

James jumps to his feet—Adam pushes him back again

Adam In such a hurry, Mr de Souza? Miss Glover will think you're an alcoholic. I get the drinks in my apartment. Would a Beefeater do you?

James (*happily jumping up*) A Beefeater—oh, lovely!

Adam Sit down! (*To Polly*) Miss Glover—Mr de Souza needs a light. (*He pours a drink*)

Polly Er—yes—of course. (*She strikes a match*)

James in his nervousness blows out the match

Oh! Sorry!

James No! No! My fault!

Polly No, no—my fault entirely. (*She drops the matches*) Oh! Hell!

Adam Tut, tut, Miss Glover—steady your nerves. What you need is a drink.

Polly The only thing wrong with our nerves is you being here, Mr Dexter.

Adam Oh, I'll go right away!

James Oh, no! No! Don't go!

James casts himself on his knees and seizes Adam

Adam He's shy, ducky. They often are these elderly bachelors.

Adam puts James back in the chair and sorts out James's cigarette and drink

Polly He's not a bachelor—he's a widower. You have been married before, haven't you, Mr de Souza?

James I, er—er—no.

James swallows some smoke and starts coughing

Adam What made you think he'd been married for God's sake?

Polly It says so on his card from the Marriage Bureau. Mrs de Souza's death was a tragedy, wasn't it?

James (*still choking*) Oh—er—er—er . . .

Adam If it was such a tragedy, why stir it up? You can see it still pains him. There, there, old fellow.

Adam pats James's head and James's toupée comes off. Adam hastily replaces it

Polly It was a tragedy because of the children.

Adam What children?

Polly His children, of course.

Adam He's got children, too?

Polly No, three.

James Ohh—huh. (*He chokes—his final and biggest choking fit*)

Adam No wonder Mr de Souza needs a wife!

Polly What he needs is a glass of water.

Polly exits to the kitchen

James Mr Dexter, sir—I know I've done wrong and you've every right to put me down, but this is going too far. I can't go on! I can't—I can't! (*He stamps his foot*)

Adam Nor can I, you can go, James.

James I can? You've finished with me?

Adam Yes—until I think of some other little service you can do me, James.

James Not again, Mr Dexter—I'm growing an old man!

Adam Lucky old you!

James exits. Polly enters with a glass of water

Polly Here you are, Mr de—where is he?

Adam 'Fraid he left.

Polly Just like that?

Adam He said he couldn't go on.

Polly It was "no, no, a thousand times no" again, I suppose.

Adam Oh, my poor ducky, if I'd have known you fancied him, I'd have kept him here—by brute force if necessary.

Polly Of course I didn't fancy him.

Adam Well, there goes Number Two your last chance. You'll have to work your way through those ninety blokes after all—starting with me.

Polly Why start with you?

Adam Well, I'm here. And you must have had some reason for keeping me here—without my clothes and all? (*He tosses the door knob*)

Polly Me keep you? If you've got any ideas like that, Mr Dexter, you can unthink them right away because—because a gentleman does not look in a lady's handbag!

Adam A lady's handbag never held anything as interesting as this. Well, what's next, Polly?

Polly I shall do exactly what you've been wanting me to do all along.

Adam Now you're talking! Come here and I'll unzip you.

Polly Mr Dexter. I'm going to marry Walter.

Adam You'll do what?

Polly Wasn't that what you were thinking?

Adam No, it was not—and you know it.

Polly Of course—you have a one-track mind.

Adam So have you—straight to the altar.

Polly exits to the bathroom. Walter, disguised, enters down the corridor and rings the bell. He is wearing a hat, dark glasses and mackintosh, and walks with knees bent

Now what? (*He shouts through the door*) Who is it?

Walter Actually, the name is de Souza!

Adam What?

Walter De Souza!

Adam (*opening the door*) De Souza? Oh, no, you missed the boat, mate. Good day to you, Mr de Souza and good-bye.

Walter (*stunned by the sight of his own pyjamas*) Uh——huh huh?

Adam What's the matter? Haven't you ever seen a man in pyjamas before, and for your information, Mr de Souza, Miss Glover has been suited. So good day to you. (*He shuts the door*)

Walter No—wait!

Adam You're wasting your time, de Souza, and mine.

Walter But actually, who's actually suited her?

Adam Actually, a perfectly frightful fellow called Waltah.

Walter I'm frightfully sorry—what am I frightfully sorry for? (*Outside*) I'm Walter! She's going to marry me!

Walter exits

The house telephone rings

Adam Hello? . . . No, but I can give her a message, Porter, Mr de Souza is fixed up. (*He hangs up*) But that's impossible, he can't even have got downstairs yet.

Polly enters from the bathroom

The house telephone rings

Polly Yes? Speaking . . . You, Walter? . . . What did you say? . . . No, of course I'm not going to marry you! . . . No, you're not to come up! . . . No, Walter—no! Walter? WALTER! (*She hangs up*) He's rung off! And he thinks I'm going to marry him. He's coming up to fetch me! And he wants his pyjamas. (*She goes to the door*)

Adam Conned by that Hayseed! I should have known it was that bloody man! (*He imitates Walter's walk*)

Polly (*coming back*) Where could he have got a crazy idea like that from?

Adam What's so crazy about it? You have been bashing away all day at this marriage thing—and where's it got you? Right back where you started from—stuck with Walter. So, for God's sake, marry the bloke.

Polly Oh, to hell with Walter—and to hell with marriage!

Adam Here! Here! To hell with marriage? Miss Glover, did I hear right?

Polly Yes. Well, go on you can unzip me now.

Adam Unzip you?

Polly Yes, you're quite safe, Mr Dexter, I'm talking about a quick flick round the mulberry bush.

Adam Just as you say, Miss Glover.

James enters and rings the bell

Polly It'll be Walter—come to fetch me! And his pyjamas, zip me up quick!

Adam But I've only just zipped you down. Go and bolt the door, while I get these off. (*He goes into the alcove*)

James opens the door with his pass key

That bloody man! And his bloody pyjamas!

Polly goes through the glass door

Polly Oh, it's you, Mr de Souza.

James Er—yes—that is, I'm just going, I've got a date.

Polly Mr de Souza—wait! Mr Dexter and I are in a terrible fix. If you could possibly help us, we'd be so grateful.

James Oh, well—if it's like that I suppose I'll have to oblige.

Walter enters, as himself

Walter Polly! Where are you?

Polly Right here, Walter, you're just the person I wanted to see.

James (*cringing*) Oh, Jiminy cricket!

Walter Oh, it's you again, is it?
Polly Oh, you know who he is?
Walter I'll say I do!
Polly Then there's no need to introduce you.
Walter You swine!
Polly Now, Walter!
Walter You over-sexed layabout, take your hands off my fiancée.
Polly No, Walter—not your fiancée. His fiancée, aren't I, darling?
Walter You? His fiancée?
Polly Yes. We're going to be married—aren't we?
Walter You and him married? Impossible?
Polly Impossible? Why?
James Last time things were different. (*He stamps his foot*)
Polly So there's nothing to keep you, is there, Walter?
Walter I simply can't see what you see in him. I mean, if he were a bull, even Old Daisy wouldn't have him.

Walter exits down the corridor

Polly Thank you so much, Mr de Souza. That was super of you.
James Super? Super? If this gets around, my reputation will be ruined!

James exits

Polly goes through the door, as Adam, wearing his own bathrobe, emerges from the alcove with the pyjamas

Polly Oh, Adam, I've got rid of Walter for good—so you can unzip me.
Adam With pleasure. (*He struggles with her zip*)
Polly Adam, zips always know when you're impatient.
Adam And zips have to learn who's master. Whoops! Alone at last.

Mrs Darcy enters in the corridor and rings the door bell. She carries the bag

I thought you'd got rid of Walter for good?
Polly It may not be him?
Adam It's always that bloody man.
Polly He wants his pyjamas! Zip me up.
Adam Not again. He'll get his pyjamas all right.
Polly Don't open the door! Don't let him in!
Adam You think I'm crazy? I'll be right back.

Mrs Darcy rings the bell impatiently

Oh, shut up! (*He feeds the pyjamas through the letter-box*) Right—now hop it, mate!
Mrs Darcy Pyjamas? What do I want with pyjamas? (*Banging on the door*) It's me—Mrs Darcy! Open the door!

Adam (*opening the door; confused*) Oh, lor—I'm sorry, Mrs D.—er, Mum . . .

Mrs Darcy Mrs Darcy to you, Mr Dexter. You don't have to look so scared—I'm not here to give you "what-for . . ." . . . I'm here to ask you —quietly and politely, like a lady—where the flaming hell are my Shirl's clothes? (*She produces the cushion*)

Adam Really, Mrs D.!

Mrs Darcy Mr Darcy always said a lady was entitled to one swear word in her lifetime—and that was mine.

Adam (*packing clothes into the bag*) Now, look, Mrs D.—sorry, Mrs Darcy—about Shirl . . .

Mrs Darcy You can forget Shirl, like she's going to forget you. Now, perhaps she'll marry Oswald like I've always wanted.

Adam Well, bully for Oswald!

Mrs Darcy *He's* a nice steady young man—works for the Co-op—got a good position in fats and lards.

Adam Well, bully for fats and lards! At least Shirl will be able to tell Stork from butter.

Mrs Darcy They *both* will the day the stork drops a little bundle in Shirl's lap.

Adam (*politely*) And I do hope they'll be very happy.

Mrs Darcy And I'm sure I hope you'll be very happy too.

Adam Don't worry about me. (*Bravely*) I expect I'll get by—carry on, carrying on, you know—and now, if you'll excuse me . . .

Mrs Darcy When you're married to Miss Polly Glover, I doubt if you'll carry on, carrying on.

Adam Married? To Polly? You shouldn't say things like that!

Mrs Darcy I'm sorry, I didn't know it was a secret. That nice Walter just told me.

Adam Nice Walter? That bloody man again! He's raving.

Mrs Darcy He said you told him so face to face and he told Admiral Glover and the Admiral's going to announce the engagement—today.

Adam But he can't! I haven't—I didn't—the Admiral must be using a periscope.

Mrs Darcy Well, I always say every dog has his day and I reckon you've had yours. Cheer up, Mr Dexter dear—you never know—it might be for better and not for worse.

Mrs Darcy exits up the corridor

Adam hurries through the door

Adam Polly, I think you'd better put your dress on.

Polly You let Walter in?

Adam No, no, here put it on.

Polly But, Adam . . .

Adam Don't argue. Hurry up.

Polly But I don't understand.

Adam Nor do I. Except that Walter's going around saying you're going to marry me.

Polly Then he's gone bonkers! Walter thinks I'm going to marry Mr de Souza. Mr de Souza just told him so face to face.

Adam Mr de Souza? What Mr de Souza?

Polly Oh, Adam—you know. The old duck in the wig, who had the choking fit. I managed to grab him and persuade him to tell Walter he was going to marry me. And he did.

Adam Hang on a minute. (*He leaves Polly and goes through the door into the other room. He is alone. He faces the audience, and begins slowly to work it all out*) The old duck in the wig—that's James. Polly thinks James is de Souza. James told Walter that he was going to marry Polly. But Walter thinks James is me. (*He realizes that he is trapped. He goes back again through the door to Polly*) Oh, my God!

Polly What's the matter? What have I done wrong?

Adam Nothing, nothing at all. Everyone digs his own grave one way or another—but by God some dig 'em deeper than others.

Polly I don't understand. I thought we were going to have a quick flick round the mulberry bush.

Adam Oh, no, we don't! Miss Glover, will you marry me?

Polly Don't be silly, come to bed.

Adam Definitely not! Will you marry me?

Polly But you don't want to get married?

Adam Inside every bachelor, there's a married man waiting to be winkled out—I'm winkled, Polly.

The outside phone rings

Polly It's working?

Adam I knew I'd paid that bill.

Polly Don't answer it!

Adam Don't fret. I've a very good idea who it is. (*He picks up the phone*) Adam Dexter speaking. Oh, yes, I was expecting your call, Admiral.

Polly Daddy? Tell him I'm not here!

Adam Yes, Admiral, your daughter's right beside me. Walter's told him we're getting married.

Polly But we're not!

Adam We are. Aye, aye, sir! The Admiral says would Saturday fortnight suit? He's not playing golf. Suits me, Admiral. You'll make the announcements tomorrow? By all means, sir—you're the expert. (*Pause*) Yes, Admiral, right away. Aye, aye, sir. (*He hangs up, salutes*) Get dressed.

Polly Now? Why?

Adam I'm afraid we'll have to wait for the honeymoon.

Polly Don't be silly!

Walter enters in the corridor. He bangs on the door and rings the bell

Who's that?

Adam Walter—come to fetch you home to Daddy.
Walter (*banging on the door*) Open up!
Polly Oh, no, we don't! (*She tries to push a chair against the door*) Help me, Adam!
Adam Stand back, Polly.
Polly What are you doing?
Adam Opening the door before he breaks it down.

Walter charges the door with his shoulder as Adam opens it, and puts out his foot. Walter hurtles in, Polly opens the next door as Walter shoots through and disappears head first down the chute. Polly and Adam close their doors and go into each other's arms, as—

the CURTAIN *falls*

FURNITURE AND PROPERTY LIST

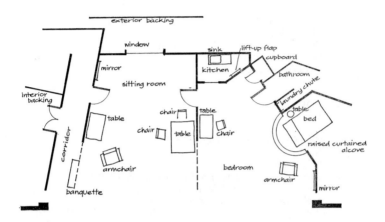

ACT I

On Stage: **SITTING-ROOM:**
Dining table. *On it:* tablecloth, ashtray, cigarettes in box
2 small chairs
Small table. *On it:* "Girlie" magazines, table lamp, box of matches
Armchair. *On it:* Polly's hat
Wall mirror
Window curtains
Power plug under small table

BEDROOM:
Double bed and bedding, with cushions
Easy chair. *Over back:* bra
Small table. *On it:* transistor
Small chair. *On it:* towel
Bedside table. *On it:* telephone
House telephone (on wall)
Laundry chute with swinging flap which covers it completely when
    not in use. The edge of the chute is waist-high and anyone falling
    down would push the swinging flap. Off stage suitable padding is
    arranged to break the actor's fall
Clothes cupboard with loose knob. *In it:* Adam's clothes, including
    4 suits, 4 shirts, 6 ties, shoes
Wall mirror
Umbrella (set near bed)

Polly's suitcase with clothes
Wall plant
Alcove curtains
Fur rug

KITCHEN:
Service hatch
Cupboards
Sink (practical)
Electric kettle
Electric coffee-pot and lead with loose wires
Whiskey, other drinks, glasses
Tea bags, sugar, teaspoons, teapot
Mugs

CORRIDOR:
Banquette

Off stage: Zip bag containing blouse, skirt, bra **(Adam)**
Bottle of milk **(Polly)**
Florist's box **(Beau)**
Glass of water and aspirin, from bathroom **(Polly)**
Zip bag (resembling Adam's) **(Mrs Darcy)**
Make-up box, from bathroom **(Polly)**
Zip bag containing pyjamas (resembling Adam's bag) **(Walter)**
Dark glasses **(Walter)**

Personal: **Walter:** pipe, matches
Adam: doorkey, cigarettes, lighter
Polly: doorkey, Marriage Bureau card
Mrs Darcy: handkerchief

ACT II

Personal: **James:** keys on ring

LIGHTING PLOT

Property fittings required: nil
Interior. An apartment. The same scene throughout

ACT I. Morning
To open: Apartment in darkness: daylight showing in corridor and exterior
Cue 1   **Polly** draws window curtains   (Page 1)
          Bring up lighting to full daylight effect

ACT II. Morning
To open: As close of Act I
No cues

EFFECTS PLOT

ACT I

Cue 1	**Walter** presses bell *Doorbell rings*	(Page 1)
Cue 2	**Walter** presses bell *Doorbell rings*	(Page 1)
Cue 3	**Polly** puts cloth down laundry chute *Chute gurgle effect*	(Page 2)
Cue 4	**Polly** turns on transistor *Light music on radio*	(Page 3)
Cue 5	**Adam** turns off transistor *Music off*	(Page 4)
Cue 6	**Adam** throws clothing down chute *Chute gurgle*	(Page 4)
Cue 7	**Adam** throws socks down chute *Chute gurgle, followed by kettle whistle*	(Page 4)
Cue 8	**Polly** drops **Adam's** jacket down chute *Chute gurgle*	(Page 6)
Cue 9	**Beau** presses bell *Doorbell rings*	(Page 13)
Cue 10	**Beau** presses bell *Doorbell rings*	(Page 14)
Cue 11	**Adam:** ". . . pants are killing me!" *House phone buzzes*	(Page 17)
Cue 12	**Adam** throws flowers down chute *Chute gurgle*	(Page 17)
Cue 13	**Walter** presses bell *Doorbell rings*	(Page 18)
Cue 14	**Beau** presses bell *Doorbell rings*	(Page 26)
Cue 15	**Walter** presses bell *Doorbell rings*	(Page 28)
Cue 16	**Adam:** ". . . once and for all." *Chute gurgle*	(Page 28)
Cue 17	**Adam** falls down chute *Chute gurgle*	(Page 29)

ACT II

ACT II

Cue 18	Adam: "... SMELLING LIKE A LOAD OF ..."	(Page 31)
	House phone buzzes	
Cue 19	Adam: "... down the lawn and that."	(Page 31)
	Choir sings	
Cue 20	Mrs Darcy presses bell	(Page 33)
	Doorbell rings	
Cue 21	Mrs Darcy: "... it's free that day?"	(Page 34)
	... the middle ...	
Cue 22	Walter presses bell	(Page 37)
	Doorbell rings	
Cue 23	Adam drops clothes down chute	(Page 41)
	Chute gurgle	
Cue 24	Walter presses bell	(Page 41)
	Doorbell rings	
Cue 25	Walter exits	(Page 43)
	House phone buzzer	
Cue 26	Polly enters	(Page 46)
	House phone buzzer	
Cue 27	James presses bell	(Page 46)
	Doorbell rings	
Cue 28	Mrs Darcy presses bell	(Page 49)
	Doorbell rings	
Cue 29	Mrs Darcy presses bell	(Page 49)
	Doorbell rings	
Cue 30	Adam: "I'm whistled, Polly".	(Page 51)
	Outside phone rings	
Cue 31	Walter presses bell	(Page 51)
	Doorbell rings	
Cue 32	Walter falls down chute	(Page 52)
	Chute gurgle	